# J. R. R.

# Tolkien

## THE MIND BEHIND
## THE RINGS

———

# MARK HORNE

NELSON
BOOKS

An Imprint of Thomas Nelson

© 2011 by Mark Horne

Previously published as part of the Christian Encounters series.

All rights reserved. No portion of this book may be reproduced, stored in a retrieval system, or transmitted in any form or by any means—electronic, mechanical, photocopy, recording, scanning, or other—except for brief quotations in critical reviews or articles, without the prior written permission of the publisher.

Published in Nashville, Tennessee, by Nelson Books, an imprint of Thomas Nelson. Nelson Books and Thomas Nelson are registered trademarks of HarperCollins Christian Publishing, Inc.

Thomas Nelson titles may be purchased in bulk for educational, business, fund-raising, or sales promotional use. For information, please e-mail SpecialMarkets@ThomasNelson.com.

Unless otherwise noted, Scripture quotations are taken from the NEW KING JAMES VERSION. © 1982 by Thomas Nelson, Inc. Used by permission. All rights reserved.

ISBN 978-0-7852-9646-1 (paperback)

**Library of Congress Cataloging-in-Publication Data**

Horne, Mark.
  J.R.R. Tolkien / Mark Horne.
        p. cm. -- (Christian encounters series)
  Includes bibliographical references.
  ISBN 978-1-59555-106-1
  1. Tolkien, J. R. R. (John Ronald Reuel), 1892-1973—Religion. 2. Authors, English—20th century—Biography. 3. Christianity and literature—Great Britain—History—20th century. 4. Christianity in literature. I. Title.
  PR6039.O32Z66137 2011
  823'.912—dc22
  [B]                                             2010040452

*Printed in the United States of America*

22 23 24 25 26 LSC 6 5 4 3 2 1

To Jennifer, Calvin, Nevin Evangeline, and Charis.

Not all those who wander are lost.

# CONTENTS

# INTRODUCTION

The middle-aged man, a war veteran, a husband, and a father, sat making marks on papers that covered his desk in his warm study. Outside his window he could see the green suburban countryside, but he could not afford the time to go outside and work in the garden that he loved, or even simply walk about, though he loved these outdoors of England. There was no time.

As with any other father, J. R. R. Tolkien needed to provide for his growing family. While he was happy being a professor at Oxford and with the work it involved, he had many financial needs as his family's provider that stretched his income to the breaking point. He needed to do more. So, when others had vacations or simply enjoyed the relatively slow summer days at Oxford, Tolkien graded exams as an "external examiner" for universities in Britain and Ireland, receiving the essay exams of students, grading them, and sending them back. He was more than qualified for the work, having acquired the advanced education that it required, but it was academia's version of manual labor. He later remembered "the everlasting weariness" of "that annual task forced on impecunious academics with children."[1]

That summer day, in the midst of the dreary boredom of marking papers, Tolkien did something that changed his life. Working diligently on marking one of many exams, Tolkien came to the bottom of a page in the exam book, expecting more handwriting to read, evaluate, and mark when he turned it over. But the next page was blank. And for some reason he took up his pen and wrote across the blank space, "In a hole in the ground there lived a hobbit."

He had no idea what a "hobbit" was. When he did define a hobbit, it would change the literary world.

J. R. R. Tolkien's *The Hobbit* and *The Lord of the Rings*— *The Fellowship of the Ring*, *The Two Towers*, and *The Return of the King*—are hugely popular. *The Hobbit* has stayed in print for eighty-five years, selling more than 140 million copies.[2] *The Lord of the Rings* trilogy has sold approximately 150 million copies[3] since the first volume was published in 1954, making the trilogy and its predecessor some of the best-known and most widely read books in all of literature. These four books have inspired numerous adaptations: feature films, video games, and television shows, including an Amazon Studios series debuting in late 2022, reported to cost more than a billion dollars to produce.[4]

While these books and products are favorites among the general public, some of his readers may not know that throughout Tolkien's life he dealt with crises and situations and responded to them in a way that honored God.

Recognizing Tolkien's faith is important to understanding his works. Being raised by his mother in the Christian faith was something he remembered—and appreciated—all his life. He was grateful to the Christians who aided her in his upbringing. As a high school and college student, he was already concerned about how his Christian faith might be involved in his artistic ambitions. He later joined with other Christian friends, especially C. S. Lewis, who were committed to artistic endeavors empowered by their Christian faith.

Possibly even more important than the Christian theological and literary influences on Tolkien's writings, the way Christianity helped him deal with the crises and losses in his life made it possible for him to write with maturity and character. The apostle Paul preached that "we must through many tribulations enter the kingdom of God" (Acts 14:22), and it was only through many tribulations that Tolkien reached the point that he could write *The Lord of the Rings* trilogy—a sequel that grew from but far surpassed his original *Hobbit*. Tolkien's faith helped him to persevere in the midst of severe losses and taught him patience as he forced himself to work at his job and support his family even as he wished he could make further progress in his writing. His faith transformed him as a person and a writer.

# BETWEEN THE SHIRE AND MORDOR, PART ONE (1892–1909)

The first nightmarishly large spider Tolkien ever encountered was not imaginary, but a real creature of the African wild.

There were many kinds of dangerous creatures even in the relatively inhabited areas of South Africa—at least when compared to the wildlife around similar houses back in England. As a three-year-old, Ronald was learning to walk and becoming interested in his family's garden. In the 1890s in interior South Africa, Ronald's learning to walk involved a great deal more anxiety for his parents and their servants. It was not uncommon to find poisonous snakes on the property amid the tall grass of Bloemfontein. Outdoors it was much less possible to keep the smaller dangerous wildlife away from homes. Even the pets could be a problem: one time a neighbor's monkey climbed into their yard and chewed up the baby Ronald's pinafores.

Running around in his family's garden, dressed all in white, he looked like a fairy or an elf, his mother said. Somehow he got far enough away from the nurse who was in charge of him that she did not see the furry, dark tarantula before it bit little Ronald. The nurse chased down the panicked, screaming child, grabbed him, and located the bite. It must have been just as traumatic for little Ronald for her to suck the poison out of the bite as receiving the bite had been in the first place. But aside from initial pain, the treatment was effective. Ronald suffered no ill effects from the tarantula's poison.

From this story, many students of Tolkien's works have thought this spider must have been the "mother" of the giant spiders of Mirkwood with whom Bilbo Baggins did battle—and later, Shelob, who nearly killed Frodo. Actually, Tolkien related that his recollections of the event were so dim that they didn't even include the spider. He only remembers the heat of the day and running in fear through the tall, dead grass.[1] Rather, he later wrote that if his portrayal of the monster spider Shelob had anything to do with "my being stung by a tarantula when a small child, people are welcome to the notion (supposing the improbable, that any one is interested). I can only say that I remember nothing about it, should not know it if I had not been told; and I do not dislike spiders particularly, and have no urge to kill them. I usually rescue those whom I find in the bath!"[2]

So, while many of Tolkien's creative invention came from his own childhood, the giant spiders of Mirkwood apparently did not. Tolkien said in a 1957 radio interview that "I put in the spiders largely because this was, you remember, primarily written for my children (at least I had them in mind)." His son Michael hated spiders. Tolkien said, "I did it to thoroughly frighten him and it did!"[3] The encounter with the tarantula may have been one of the few experiences in Tolkien's life that accidentally matched his stories, rather than influenced them. As we will see, Tolkien's memories of events that affected his creative life came from a little later when he was living in the English countryside, giving names to people that came from fairy tales. He was probably too young in Africa to be greatly influenced by life there. The main effect of his early childhood in the dusty plains of South Africa was probably to give him a great love for the green hills and woods of England when he finally got to experience them a little later.

———

J. R. R. Tolkien was born in South Africa on January 3, 1892. His full name was John Ronald Reuel Tolkien, and most of his early life he was known simply as "Ronald." His second middle name came from the middle name of his father, Arthur Reuel Tolkien. His first name was in honor of his paternal grandfather, John Benjamin Tolkien. Arthur wanted to call his son by one of the two names from his side of the family; however, his wife, Mabel, née Suffield, preferred to refer to her son as Ronald, and that is what he ended up being called in most of his early life. On February 17, 1894, a second son was born to Arthur and Mabel. They named him Hilary Arthur Reuel Tolkien.

## FROM SOUTH AFRICA TO ENGLAND

Bloemfontein, located in the northern interior of South Africa, is now a modern city with over a half million people in the metro area. But when Tolkien was an infant growing into a toddler, it was much more like a frontier town, where wild animals roamed nearby. The house was on a high plain, windswept and woodless. What shade Tolkien found in his yard came from fir, cypress, and cedar saplings placed there by his father in an attempt to create a kind of oasis in the desert.[4] The town was located in an independent country called the Orange Free State, which was dominated by settlers of Dutch ancestry.

His father had relocated to South Africa initially for economic reasons since he belonged to a family of flagging fortunes. Arthur's father, John Benjamin, had been a seller of pianos and music before he had gone bankrupt in 1877. Arthur became a bank manager and found that moving to South Africa held much more promise for financial advancement than remaining in England. After he relocated to South Africa, his fiancée, Mabel, followed him there and married him in Cape Town before moving inland to their new home.

From the beginning of Arthur's move, it was an open question as to whether it would be a lifelong situation or a temporary residency. Mabel, once she arrived and experienced life in Africa, began to strongly hope that their stay would only be temporary. She did not like the climate and longed for the cooler weather she remembered back in England. She also believed the heat was damaging her older son's health. Arthur, on the other hand, began to feel that he had found a new home and might never live in England again. He hoped that Ronald would adapt to the climate as he grew older. In the meantime, his mother took him and his younger brother on a long train trip to the coast to get them to moister, cooler air.[5]

In time, the family turned their attention to a long-planned return visit to England. Mabel and her children disembarked in April 1895 without Arthur since business and financial pressures prevented him from leaving at the same time. Watching his father paint *A. R. Tolkien* on the family's trunk became one of Tolkien's few clear recollections of the man.[6]

Mabel and the boys stayed with her father in his home in Birmingham, the second-largest populated center in England. The plan for Arthur to travel from South Africa to join them was delayed because he developed rheumatic fever and was too sick to make the voyage. They needed to wait until he was healthy again.

Yet Arthur never became healthy again. By January 1896, Mabel was planning to return to South Africa in order to care for her husband.[7] But, before she could do so, the disease caused a brain hemorrhage. Arthur Tolkien was already buried five thousand miles away by the time Mabel learned that he was dead. No one in the family could even afford to visit the grave site.[8]

The most obvious and earliest tribulation Tolkien faced that had a direct impact on him was losing his father at such a young age. Many biographers simply mention that it happened and move on to other steps in Tolkien's development as an author. But Tolkien's religious imagination and faith would have almost certainly been very different if his father had lived.

Also, the fact that Tolkien lost his father at a young age seems to have significance to him not only as a person but also as a creative writer. Interesting studies show that people who have lost one or both parents are highly represented among creative people.[9] The list of writers who lost one or both parents during childhood includes Dante, Jonathan Swift, Voltaire, Jean-Jacques Rousseau, Edward Gibbon, William Wordsworth, Samuel Taylor Coleridge, Lord Byron, John Keats, Alexandre Dumas, George Sand, Edgar Allan Poe, Charles Baudelaire, Fyodor Dostoyevsky, Leo Tolstoy, and Charlotte, Emily, and Anne Brontë.[10] A researcher once took a standard textbook selection of English and French poets and found that 30 percent of them had lost their fathers to death or abandonment very early in life.[11] Other research by a doctoral student took a common textbook on French literature and found that seventeen out of thirty-five writers had, through death or divorce, lost one or both parents.[12]

Many children without fathers suffer in overwhelmingly negative ways, but others have the internal resources so that they rise to the occasion. It may well be that being without a father was a factor in Tolkien's artistic accomplishment.

## ENGLAND AND THE WORLD OF A YOUNG BOY'S IMAGINATION

Tolkien remembered very little of his life in South Africa. However, it is clear that the contrasting climate and geography of England made a big impression on him—one that worked its way into his fiction. On a limited budget, his mother managed to find a place to rent in a small town called Sarehole. There, a mile outside Birmingham, Tolkien discovered the beauty of the English countryside—his first "Shire." Here, as a small boy, with his younger brother, Tolkien spent a great deal of time playing and exploring. One can see his later fiction getting its start even here in a youngster's imagination.

The ogres that attacked and harassed the two boys (as they would describe it) are one example of a childhood incident showing up in later fiction. The best way to understand how seriously the boys took "the ogres" is to read a letter that younger brother Hilary later wrote. One day Mabel decided to take lunch to her boys. She had allowed them to go out and "blackberry" in a place locals called "the Dell." So she made the lunches and went in search of the boys. Their house in Sarehole Mill stood with a few others, but the surrounding countryside made it easy to overlook how near they were to Birmingham. They rarely saw much traffic on the road other than a farmer's cart or the wagon of a tradesman. So Mabel walked across the road and crossed a meadow to the River Cole. There stood the Sarehole Mill, an old brick building that had been used for grinding corn for three hundred years but was now used for grinding bone to produce phosphates to add to manure.

There was a narrow path here, leading through land owned by the miller and on to the Dell. While Mabel stayed on the path as she was supposed to, her boys had not been so respectful of the property of the landowner. Hilary Tolkien wrote that the miller was not very appreciative of the boys because they "traipsed off after corncockles and other pretty things."[13] As Mabel came to the Dell, she called out to her boys, who had not seen their mother approach. The results were immediate and dramatic: both boys began running away from her through the brush without even looking up. Mabel's voice when she yelled was, in the perception of the young Tolkien boys, deep enough to be a man's voice. They thought she was the "White Ogre" come to harass them for straying on his land rather than keeping to the narrow path. The "White Ogre" was the local mill worker who earned his name because he was constantly covered in white bone dust from the inside of the mill. He was relatively mild, since he merely yelled at them to get off his land or away from the mill.

Their other enemy was worse, and they called him the "Black Ogre." The boys loved to explore a sandpit they found lined with trees but had to deal with his opposition to their trespassing. One day eight-year-old Ronald discovered an area with some mushrooms growing and picked them. The property owner chased off Tolkien, earning a nickname in the process. The property owner would take their shoes and socks when they went into the river to play and would spank the boys when they were forced to approach him to get their footwear back.

As a frightening guardian of the mushrooms, the Black Ogre was moved to Hobbiton, not as a monster, but as a wise and kind, though fearsome, hobbit:

"I know these fields and this gate!" he [Pippin] said. "This is Bamfurlong, old Farmer Maggot's land. That's his farm away there in the trees."

"One trouble after another!" said Frodo, looking nearly as much alarmed as if Pippin had declared the lane was the slot leading to a dragon's den. The others looked at him in surprise.

"What's wrong with old Maggot?" asked Pippin. "He's a good friend to all the Brandybucks. Of course, he's a terror to trespassers, and keeps ferocious dogs—but after all, folk down here are near the border and have to be more on their guard."

"I know," said Frodo. "But all the same," he added with a shamefaced laugh, "I am terrified of him and his dogs. I have avoided his farm for years and years. He caught me several times trespassing after mushrooms, when I was a youngster in Brandy Hall. On the last occasion he beat me, and then took me and showed me to his dogs. 'See, lads,' he said, 'next time this young varmint sets foot on my land, you can eat him. Now see him off!' They chased me all the way to the Ferry. I have never got over the fright—though I daresay the beasts knew their business and would not really have touched me."[14]

Tolkien's childhood involved several moves based on financial necessity and educational needs. According to his own recollections, the desirability of these homes was based on whether they were in the English countryside, which he loved, or if they were in places of suburban or urban development, which he strongly disliked. The basis of Tolkien's love for trees and nature over his dislike for machinery was set early in his life. The reader finds virtually all mention of "machinery" in *The Lord of the Rings* is associated with villains like Saruman and Sauron in the pursuit of power and the enslavement of others.

In these early years, Tolkien's mother homeschooled both boys. She began teaching Tolkien Latin and he loved it, so she started French lessons as well, and while he didn't find French as lovely sounding as Latin and English,[15] he clearly showed an aptitude with languages that would later become his academic career. It is noteworthy that Tolkien studied these subjects under his mother's tutelage when he was around seven years old.

Tolkien also remembered the influence of certain stories in his young years. He loved the children's novels by George Macdonald, *The Princess and the Goblin* and *The Princess and Curdie*. He would later come to judge much of the Victorian author's writings as far too allegorical and moralistic, but at a young age he found them quite enjoyable. They influenced his imagination much as they did for the child who would grow up to be his friend—C. S. Lewis. One can't help but wonder how much the Mines of Moria would have figured into *The Fellowship of the Ring* without these stories of an underground goblin kingdom threatening human miners.

Though Tolkien had fond memories of his childhood, this time period involved another change in fortunes for his mother, his brother, and himself. Only a few years after the death of his father, Tolkien experienced separation from much of his extended family.

## A MOVE OF FAITH

Though the reports of her faith journey lack detail, it is known that regular worship and participation in church became much more important to Mabel in the years following her husband's death. As a single mother responsible for the raising of two young boys, she would find herself more aware of her need to live by faith. As Mabel became more involved in the Anglican Church, she found herself most nourished in the Anglo-Catholic portion of that national denomination. The Anglican Church could be classified in three main categories, "low church," "high church," and "broad church." Broad church was and is simply those who see themselves between the other two groups—though it can also refer to theological "modernism" or "liberalism." The "low church" Anglicans are the typical Evangelicals who see their heritage as distinctively Protestant, tend toward simpler prayer book worship, and emphasize the doctrine of justification by faith. "High church" refers to those who emphasize the identity of the Anglican Church in continuity with the early church and the succession of bishops and who would typically use a more elaborate liturgy.

As someone who began to study and care passionately about Christianity and the church, Mabel Tolkien found herself growing in a "high church" direction. Despite the distance she had to walk with her young boys, she went to an Anglo-Catholic church to worship on Sunday. But eventually she was led to visit a slum area in the middle of Birmingham, where she entered St. Anne's on Alcester Street—a Roman Catholic church. Soon thereafter, in 1900, when Tolkien was eight years old, Mabel officially became a member of the Roman Catholic Church and brought her boys into it with her. (St. Anne's had been the epicenter from 1849 to 1852 of the ministry of John Newman, an Anglican churchman who promoted the high church within Anglicanism until his switch to the Roman Catholic Church.)

His mother's conversion may have protected Tolkien's upbringing as a Christian. Many of Mabel's relatives were, in the terminology of England, "nonconformists." What this meant is that they were outside the official Church of England, the Anglican Church. Several of her relatives were nonconformists because they were Methodists, while several on the Tolkien side of the family were Baptists. However, the term could even cover aberrant nonevangelical groups who rejected basic Christian doctrine. Mabel's father, brought up as Methodist, had become a Unitarian who denied the essentials of the Christian faith, including the identity of God in Trinity as Father, Son, and the Holy Spirit, and the deity of Jesus, his resurrection, and the atoning efficacy of his death on the cross. Mabel made the decision to have her priest and friend, Father Francis Morgan, appointed the boys' guardian in the event of her death rather than appointing any family members, thus ensuring they would be brought up in the Roman Catholic faith.

Mabel's conversion to Roman Catholicism was the cause of another kind of family loss for the Tolkien boys. While there is no record of any of Mabel's Methodist siblings and other relatives disowning her Unitarian father, they did ostracize Mabel for her religion and cut off what financial help they were giving to her and her two boys. According to some accounts, the anger and opposition, in addition to impoverishing her, hurt her health.[16] But she remained steadfast and gave instruction to her children. Tolkien's first communion was on Christmas 1903 when he was almost twelve years old.

Remembering her death years later, Tolkien was still haunted by the additional burden she bore of isolation from family. He described her as "worn out with persecution, poverty, and, largely consequent, disease, in the effort to hand on to us small boys the faith." And specifically he said he remembered "the tiny bedroom she shared with us in rented rooms in a postman's cottage at Rednal, where she died alone."[17]

# BETWEEN THE SHIRE AND MORDOR, PART TWO (1892–1909)

A s early as the age of seven, Tolkien tried to pass entrance exams to gain entrance to King Edward's school, his father's alma mater. However, he did not get in until a year later. Despite the problems Mabel faced when she began going to the Roman Catholic Church, she found a relative on the Tolkien side of the family who paid the cost of her son's education.

## FORMAL SCHOOLING

King Edward's school has a history going back to 1552, when King Edward VI founded it by royal charter. While entrance now begins with boys who have turned eleven, in Tolkien's day one could become a student much earlier. It was a place of grand architecture reflecting its long history. (It since has moved to a different location.)

Mabel and the boys moved into Birmingham, where a train line was nearby to get Tolkien to King Edward's on a daily basis. Here, in a small rental house, they lived within sight of ugly factory smokestacks[1]—a Mordor-like place. The family soon had to move again in Birmingham, but the environment didn't change for the better.

Early in 1902, the family relocated again. Mabel found a Roman Catholic parish where she felt she was being ministered to in the Birmingham Oratory founded by John Henry Newman. There were priests to minister to her, a Catholic school where her boys could receive a Catholic education, and a nearby house to rent. This meant that the ten-year-old Tolkien was pulled out of King Edward's school so that he could attend the Oratory's St. Philip's Grammar School.[2] Perhaps more important to Mabel, and ultimately more important to the boys, was that she found a priest and confessor whom she believed she could trust, Father Francis Morgan.

Tolkien only spent a few months at St. Philip's before Mabel realized that it was an academic dead end for her children. The classes were crowded and expectations were low. The school was warehousing students for eventual factory jobs.[3] She pulled them both out and began homeschooling them again while working to get them back at King Edward's. Her teaching paid off for Tolkien. The next year he won a scholarship and began attending King Edward's again.[4] His brother, Hilary, however, did not pass the entry exams and had to be homeschooled another year before joining him at the school. Tolkien remained and excelled at King Edward's during his high school years, not only getting a great foundation for a brilliant academic career but also making the most important friendships of his youth.

## THE SECOND ORPHANING

In April 1904, shortly after Tolkien's twelfth birthday, his mother fell ill and was hospitalized. Doctors diagnosed Mabel as having diabetes. While the disease involves a genetic predisposition, research indicates an environmental trigger. Something in the Tolkien household had fulfilled the necessary condition. Both boys were sick in bed at the beginning of the year with measles, followed by whooping cough, and then, in Hilary's case, pneumonia.[5] Somewhere in the process of taking care of them, Mabel developed this dangerous condition in a time before the disease could be treated with insulin injections. She was hospitalized but released by the beginning of summer.

Mabel could not possibly resume her job as full-time mother and keeper of the household right away. She needed more time to recover. And recovery would, she knew, only be temporary. Eventually, but invariably, diabetes would be fatal.[6]

A recovery period was arranged by the family friend and priest Father Francis Morgan. They moved to Rednal, now a suburb of Birmingham, though at the time it was less developed. John Henry Newman had established a retreat there for priests, and next to the property lived a couple who would rent the Tolkien family two rooms and cook meals for them. So that summer, the boys were back in Shire-like country, living with their mother and enjoying the English countryside. When the summer was over, Tolkien had to begin classes at King Edward's again. They continued to live in the rented rooms, and young Tolkien made a long commute every weekday.

Even with this arrangement, Mabel did not live very long. She fell into a coma and died six days later on November 14, 1904.

Interestingly, as we have already seen in the case of the death of Tolkien's father, orphans have been historically highly represented in creative fields. An examination of 699 persons to whom the *Encyclopedia Britannica* had given more than one column's worth of space shows that, in this sample from different nations and times, "a quarter had lost one parent before the age of 10, more than two thirds before age 15, and half before they were 21."[7]

A lifelong consequence of the way Mabel died was that it secured her place in Tolkien's memory as somewhat of a martyr. As far as he was concerned, if Mabel's family had not abandoned her and if they had provided her with the financial support a widow should have received, then she most likely would not have died so young. Tolkien later gave a terse summary of his mother to his son Michael, when he was away serving during World War II. He wrote that she "was a gifted lady of great beauty and wit, greatly stricken by God with grief and suffering, who died in youth [at 34] of a disease hastened by persecution for her faith—died in the postman's cottage at Rednal, and is buried at Bromsgrove."[8]

Amid all the personal and world tragedies that he lived through, Tolkien's faith did not waver—Tolkien believed that he and his brother had been the beneficiaries of his mother's willing self-sacrifice. Nine years after his mother died, he not only called her a martyr but wrote that "it was not to everybody that God grants so easy a way to His great gifts as He did to Hilary and myself, giving us a mother who killed herself with labor and trouble to ensure us keeping the faith."[9]

## CHILD OF THE CHURCH AND FIRST LOVE

With his mother gone, there was even less connection with many of Tolkien's family members on his mother's or his father's side. Just as Mabel had found needed support in the Roman Catholic Church, she entrusted the boys into the church's care when she was gone. In her will, she made her friend and spiritual helper, Father Francis Morgan, the legal guardian of her boys. He would now look after them and provide for them. He even sometimes used his own private funds to supplement what little the boys had inherited. The descendant of Welsh and Spanish families, Morgan had a private income from his family's business of importing and selling sherry.

Morgan, however, did not see a way to keep the boys at the Oratory's dorms—which were far too crowded—and was willing for them to live with family but was unsure who to trust to not take them away from the Roman Catholic Church. According to Tolkien's biographer, Humphrey Carpenter, "Already there had been some talk of contesting Mabel's will and of sending the boys to a Protestant boarding-school."[10] The will was never contested, but Morgan had to be careful. He found that one of Mabel's sisters-in-law, Beatrice Suffield, did not have strong religious convictions and lived near the Oratory in Birmingham. Herself a recent widow, she was in need of money, so she rented them her upstairs bedroom.[11]

This was a rather dreary move for Tolkien. He hated the view from his room, which was virtually all rooftops and then smokestacks beyond, showing only a tiny glimpse of the English countryside far out of reach—a place he now associated with his departed mother.[12] Once again, he was in Mordor and unable to even imagine a return to the Shire. Staying with a relative did not do much to ease the suffering. While Beatrice Suffield was safe because she was not zealously anti-Catholic, she also proved to be rather lacking in empathy. It was a lodging place rather than a home.

The boys' real home was the Oratory. They would walk there early in the morning to assist Father Morgan in serving Mass and then walk to King Edward's school together. Tolkien got respite from the city every summer because Father Morgan took the boys on vacation in Lyme Regis, a coastal town in West Dorset on the southern end of England. There Tolkien got a little more of the English countryside that he loved, as well as the sea.

It was on one of those trips that Father Morgan learned of how alienated Tolkien felt living with his aunt.[13] She had even burned his mother's personal papers and correspondence, claiming it never occurred to her that the boys might want to save them.[14] So in 1908, Father Morgan decided to find a better place and ended up moving the boys to a house only a block from the Oratory where they could rent rooms from a Mrs. Faulkner.

It is not clear if Tolkien and his brother deemed this much of an improvement. However, it was to make an immense difference in Tolkien's life. Also rooming at the house was a nineteen-year-old young woman, Edith Bratt. She was an accomplished pianist who became friends with Tolkien though she was three years his senior. Tolkien was attracted to her artistic talent and her engaging personality, and as time wore on, they began to find private ways to communicate that would not be considered outright inappropriate. Tolkien's room was directly above Edith's. They found they could actually talk to each other while leaning out their windows at night without awakening the others in the house.[15]

Edith, born to a single mother, had never known her father. Her mother had died by 1908, which is why she was renting a room and was on her own. Tolkien later wrote of "the dreadful sufferings of childhoods, from which we rescued one another, but could not wholly heal the wounds that later often proved disabling."[16] He felt drawn to her based on a shared experience of loss. Eventually they began taking walks or going bicycling together, though they made a point of not letting anyone at their house know that they were spending time together. When they weren't walking or bicycling, they would arrange to meet in a tea shop.

The two decided in the summer of 1909 that they were in love.[17]

However, it was far too early in Tolkien's life for him to do anything about his love and loyalty for Edith. Father Morgan would see it only as a foolish attraction to distract him from his academic prospects.

## AN EARLY LOVE FOR LANGUAGE

One of Tolkien's gifts that became more and more obvious was his capacity for, and love of, language. Not only did Tolkien learn other languages early, with his mother teaching him Latin and French, but he later remembered an interest in words and their origins.

One of his earliest memories of the way fantasy and language influenced him was his attempt to write a story about a dragon. While accounts vary, he wrote in a 1955 letter to W. H. Auden that he remembered attempting this story around the age of seven and being told by his mother that "green great dragon" was not right; it had to be "great green dragon." He said he was intrigued at the time and still remained intrigued as to why language had to work in this way.[18] He also remembered an early "fascination" with Welsh names "even if only seen on coal-trucks."[19] Later, when he was in the care of Father Francis Morgan, Tolkien strove to study more Spanish because of Father Morgan's Spanish heritage. Tolkien said it was the only Romance language he found to be as pleasurable in its cadences and rhythms as the Germanic and Old English languages he grew to love.

As a boy, Tolkien began working with friends to make up

new private languages. He was not the originator of such a concept. He first heard others speaking in a language they dubbed "Animalic," which emphasized animal names.[20] He joined this hobby and began working on others. While he referred to it later as his "secret vice," it was not really secret; he told anyone who was interested. Unlike other children, rather than getting bored with such a hobby, Tolkien grew more interested from adolescence into adulthood.

This growing interest in language began to shape and motivate his school performance. While Tolkien may have started at a slow speed according to the expectations of the British middle class in the early twentieth century, his reentry into King Edward's with a scholarship shows that he had improved. There he became proficient in the school's bedrock curriculum of Greek and Latin and placed first in the "Fifth Class" (the grade under the freshman class) in 1905.[21] However, his proficiency in Greek and Latin meant that eventually he would grow bored with them and want to move on to other languages.

Right behind him in second place was Christopher Wiseman, a year younger than Tolkien and the son of a Methodist minister.[22] While Wiseman and Tolkien became friends in part because they shared many of the same intellectual interests and found mutual encouragement in each other, they were also comrades in rugby—a sport that Tolkien loved—and played on the same house team.[23]

For many readers, the closest they will have come to experiencing something of Tolkien's school background is reading J. K. Rowling's fictional Harry Potter series. Tolkien was a member of one of four "houses" in the school, and he participated vigorously in the intramural rugby games in which these houses competed.

Wiseman shared Tolkien's interest in language and shared in his development of private languages. They both found themselves to be great companions for each other, both interested in athletic and intellectual attainments. Wiseman was also talented in music and wrote a composition while still a young man that was included in a Methodist hymnal.[24]

Tolkien balanced athletic and academic interests, with his love of languages driving him to learn more. In 1908, sixteen-year-old Tolkien was reading Greek and Chaucer in the original Middle English.[25] Academically, he made high marks in German, while studying Anglo-Saxon and Gothic on his own.[26] At this point he began to show a strong preference for the Germanic rather than the Classical—a preference that would cause him some initial problems a few years later in Oxford. Perhaps Tolkien simply liked to stand out from the standard curriculum. As biographer John Garth puts it, "Against the Classicist ethos drummed into King Edward's schoolboys he played the outsider with verve."[27] He extolled the superiority of the Icelandic *Volsunga Saga* with its story of Sigurd slaying the dragon, and was bold enough to deliver addresses in Gothic at the annual Latin debates.[28] While much of this was done in 1910 before his second attempt at the exams, the same interests and occupations were already present when he was studying a year earlier.

One might think that such ability meant Tolkien would

have no problem winning a needed Oxford scholarship. But that was far from the case. In order to do well enough on his entry exams to win a scholarship, Tolkien needed to study hard in the Classical heritage, which did not hold much interest to him by this time. It was much more fun to work on a private language or go to a tea shop with Edith. So, getting into Oxford proved to be difficult for Tolkien. In his first attempt in 1909, he did not do well enough to gain a place.

## LEGENDS OF A LOST WORLD

While there always would be setbacks and obstacles, in his time at King Edward's, Tolkien set a course that would determine the direction of much of his life. He had the love of languages that would remain with him and shape his career. He had his romantic interest in Edith Bratt that, though it would be put on hold for a few years, would lead him to marriage and children. He had a lifelong friendship in Christopher Wiseman.

Tolkien claimed to have a recurring dream from his early childhood—perhaps better described as a nightmare. In it there was a "Great Wave, towering up and coming in ineluctably over the trees and green fields."[29] Tolkien described his dream as what "some might call an Atlantis complex."[30] Before writing of it in private correspondence, he gave the dream to a hero in *The Return of the King*. Faramir dreamed of it as what happened to Numenor or Westernesse: "The great dark wave climbing over the green lands and above the hills, and coming on, darkness unescapable. I often dream of it."[31]

For anyone familiar with Tolkien's life, it is tempting to see the wave as prophetic. Tolkien's family had been swept away from him in early life. When his mother was taken away, he himself saw the "trees and green fields" of his childhood home swept away for a location of brick and smoke. Tolkien lived to see much else he knew as home swept away by the tides of change. In a sense, the history of Middle-earth was his own version of an Atlantis myth—the legendary recollection of a lost world.

# COMING OF AGE
# (1910–1911)

**W**atch this, Edith," the teenage boy said to the pretty girl sitting across from him as he picked up a sugar lump from the bowl at their table.[1] To any onlooker, he appeared handsome and athletic—partially due to a hearty commitment to playing rugby with his schoolmates. But there were no onlookers here on the second floor.

The couple's favorite Birmingham tea shop had a balcony overlooking the street below. From there they sat and sipped tea and watched the foot traffic beneath them, talking of trivial things.

The boy was too mischievous to merely watch. He had just spotted a large, flowery hat parading below. It presented a tempting target for a teenage boy who wanted to impress a girl. "Don't do it, Ronald," said Edith, in a tone that did nothing to make Tolkien hesitate in executing his plan. He gently tossed the lump of sugar at the wide brim passing on the street.

Miss!

"Oh no," whispered Edith, ducking back behind the balcony rail.

But she didn't need to worry. The sugar lump hit the street silently, and neither the woman underneath the hat nor anyone else near her noticed it. Tolkien grabbed another fast, before the hat was out of range. "This time I'll make it."

He reached his target. Tolkien grinned and Edith giggled as the lady walked away with an extra sugar lump decorating the brim of her colorful hat.

"My turn," said Edith.

After they had emptied the sugar bowl playing their game and sweetening the headgear of several lady pedestrians, Edith and Tolkien moved to the next table, where a full sugar bowl would allow them to play another round. With no one there to stop them, they were free to have fun.

All was innocent fun; however, the problem was Tolkien needed to be studying hard in order to win a scholarship to Oxford. When he took the entrance exams for the first time in 1909, he failed to do well enough. Now he was about to turn nineteen. If he did not succeed this time, there would be no third chance. Everything his mother had strived for to better his education and to give him opportunities to rise above their impoverished circumstances was at stake.

Understandably, those concerned about Tolkien did not want him spending time dallying with a young woman—especially one three years older. However, Tolkien was prone to seek escape. Between games with his male friends and private time with Edith, he overextended himself.

## ROMANCE AND AUTHORITY

Tolkien not only overextended himself in the years when he was attempting to get into Oxford, but he did so in such a way that brought him into trouble with his guardian, Father Francis Morgan, a man whom he loved, respected, and admired. His conflict with Father Morgan demonstrates rather vividly what a different world existed in England before World War I. Despite the fact that Tolkien lived in the twentieth century, the challenges he faced as a young man in love facing dire risks and limited options are reminiscent of the kinds of economic situations one reads about in a Jane Austen novel.

One must remember Tolkien was poor in the context of the British middle class. While there were many people who were worse off than he was in British society, not many of such people would be going to the same school he attended or have the same class of friends that Tolkien had gained. As a teenager who had intelligence and ability, successfully competing for a limited number of Oxford scholarships was essential to his future success. The fact that he had such gifts made it the obvious direction he should pursue, but they did not guarantee that he would be able to reach his goal. Success required concentrated effort. But tea shops, making up languages, and other diversions with friends were getting in the way.

There were some aspects of Edith that would make it easy to understand why a guardian would worry that Tolkien was headed in the wrong direction. While Edith was accomplished in music for her age, she did not share Tolkien's intellectual interests or have a corresponding educational background.

Knowing Father Morgan would not approve of their relationship, once they admitted to each other their mutual love, Tolkien and Edith tried all the more to hide their time together from their neighbors and the landlady. But this, not surprisingly, ended in failure. The priest found out that his ward, who was supposed to be studying for what might have been the most important tests of his life, was courting a Protestant woman three years older—and who lived in the same house. Father Morgan confronted Tolkien, demanded that the relationship end, and relocated Tolkien and his brother yet again.[2]

It was in the middle of this drama and trauma in 1909 that Tolkien had to take his entrance exams for Oxford—a test unlikely to include any material on "obscure languages, philology, or linguistic invention,"[3] the topics that Tolkien loved. The irony is that if distractions were the cause of Tolkien's failure to win a scholarship, it may well be that the stress caused by Father Morgan's outrage over Edith was the real reason for his troubles rather than Edith herself. In later years Tolkien only blamed himself for not doing well enough to win a scholarship that year. He wrote, "I was clever, but not industrious or single-minded: a large part of my failure was due to simply not working (at least not on classics) because I was studying something else: Gothic and what-not."[4] Understandably, Tolkien entered into 1910 quite depressed—and started a diary dedicated to expressing his gloom to himself.[5] His life became worse before it got better.

Given Tolkien's love of language outside the popular classics, his explanation for his insufficient performance on the exams is plausible. But it is also reasonable that Father Morgan would attribute his failure to do well on his tests to his involvement with Edith. So one can imagine his reaction when he heard that Tolkien was still seeing the young lady.

Tolkien, however, had not intended any disobedience. Father Morgan had not expressly said that he could never see her. He had only forbidden the romantic relationship. Yet, because they knew it would bother him, they had met secretly. They exchanged birthday gifts and talked about Edith's plans to relocate farther away where they wouldn't be able to see each other so easily—which they both knew was better for them. But this meeting was reported, and Father Morgan plainly told Tolkien that he was not to communicate with or see her again except to say good-bye when she moved. There would be no contact until Tolkien turned twenty-one and was no longer under guardianship. Worse, even the exception was taken away. Tolkien met Edith accidentally a couple of times and dared to speak to her. Father Morgan discovered this, treated it as intentional disobedience, and threatened to end Tolkien's educational career unless he never spoke to or saw her again.

Tolkien obeyed. Authority meant something in pre–World War I England, and it was backed with real economic power. Economically dependent on Father Morgan as his guardian,

Tolkien was also truly respectful of and loyal to him. As someone who was self-consciously loyal to romantic medieval literature as well as heroic epics, Tolkien may have been prepared to regard Father Morgan's ban on contact as a special test that he must pass in order to prove his love to Edith. As Joseph Pearce has written, such works of literature "were the roots, the archetypes, of Tolkien's view of romantic love, a view which found expression in his own self-denial during the three years of separation from Edith."[6]

The day Edith walked to the train station to leave for Cheltenham, he spotted her leaving but never spoke to her. He would not communicate with her or see her or know what was happening in her life, in submission to Father Morgan's orders, until he turned twenty-one, three years later—with one exception when he got special permission to write her the first Easter she was gone and to receive a reply.[7]

## BOY'S LIFE

Edith's complete departure from his life left Tolkien with the space to focus on preparing for his next and last opportunity to take the entrance exams. Now that they were completely separated, Tolkien threw himself into a life with male friends in sports, in fellowship, and in academic pursuits. He basically adapted to a life that had no room for a woman. During his student days at Oxford, Tolkien's friends did not even learn of Edith's existence until he was almost married to her. Tolkien now plunged into school life with no other outside distractions.

As before, he was still not as devoted to studying as he felt he should be, still having many other interests to distract him. In the month following Edith's departure, he attended a theater production of J. M. Barrie's *Peter Pan*. While, by itself, this may not seem noteworthy, the time he spent writing poetry in the next few years shows that Barrie's construct of Neverland influenced Tolkien's own mythical writing.[8] Writing poetry was another interest that would occupy his time along with his experiments in language creation.

Whatever his distractions, Tolkien studied sufficiently in the latter half of 1910 to do well enough in his exams to secure a place at Oxford. What he won was not the scholarship he had hoped for, but rather an "exhibition." This meant less money but still enough for Tolkien to afford to attend.

Having finally made his way past his most important academic test, he now faced much less pressure in his last months at King Edward's. He found plenty to do to occupy his time—things that, while they may have seemed more like recreation to him, influenced his life. Tolkien was made librarian at King Edward's, an office that was given to a senior every year. Tolkien made his friend Christopher Wiseman his assistant and brought in another friend, Vincent Trought.[9]

Together these young men, with other friends, made the library a headquarters for an informal club. Robert Quilter Gilson, the son of the school headmaster, was included. Later, Geoffrey Bache Smith also joined. While there were other members, including Wilfrid Hugh Payton and more who joined later, these students formed the center of what became known as the "Tea Club" and later the "Tea Club and Barrovian Society," or T.C.B.S.[10] The name started naturally enough with the practice of enjoying tea together. Later they began to frequent a tearoom in a Birmingham department store, Barrow's Stores, thus providing for an elaboration of their name. There they sat in an alcove known as the "Railway Carriage."[11] These boys came to dominate the cultural life of the school—taking it away from others they felt were far less interesting.[12]

While rugby was an important shared interest, the T.C.B.S. was mainly about boys with disparate academic interests sharing their knowledge and studies with one another so that they would inspire the others in their own pursuits. Tolkien thus shared what he was learning and reading in his studies of northern European languages and legends. He recited for them the Norse *Volsunga Saga*,[13] in which a dwarf is featured with a treasure horde and a magic ring. The Norse myths Tolkien found so fascinating even featured dwarves as underground metalworkers.[14] He also spent time reciting to his friends from *Beowulf* and the Middle English poem "The Pearl" and developed a special love for *Sir Gawain and the Green Knight*.

His friends in the T.C.B.S. found Tolkien's contributions rewarding. All of them had their own contributions to make to their meetings. Christopher Wiseman was a musician with an interest in the hard sciences and a gift for mathematics. Robert Gilson's mother had fostered in him a general love for art, including Renaissance and eighteenth-century painting. His passion was drawing and design, and he eventually came to hope to represent the culture of the T.C.B.S. by producing a book of designs.[15] Vincent Trought was a lover of the Romantics and a skilled poet for his age. Sadly, Trought died of illness while Tolkien was in Oxford. Geoffrey Bache Smith was younger than the others and had a special interest in more modern literature. He pushed the T.C.B.S. members into attempts to write their own poetry.[16]

Of all of these young men, only Christopher Wiseman lived more than a few years. But at the time, none of them realized what was ahead, and they inspired one another to pursue their various interests. For Tolkien, once he passed his exams for Oxford in December, there was very little formal academic pressure for him to worry about. Nevertheless, with the social reinforcement he received from his peers, and his own burning curiosity, Tolkien continued to pursue his own studies. At this time he made another literary discovery. As he wrote to W. H. Auden in 1955, "I was immensely attracted by something in the air of the *Kalevala*, even in Kirby's poor translation."[17] He resolved to learn Finnish in order to read it in the original collection of legendary stories—though he was not able to fulfill that wish until he was at Oxford.

# GROWING UP IN OXFORD
# (1911–1914)

Tolkien sat at his desk, alone in his room, the Anglo-Saxon text open before him.[1] But he found it easy not to look at its pages. Even though he found the language genuinely interesting—much more so than the Latin and Greek plays he'd been expected to study the previous year—he still found it hard to concentrate. More than once he relit his pipe and stared at his window. The restless scholar worked on and off for a bit until about ten minutes to nine, when he began to hear a distant roar, the collective rebel yell of students in the streets of the town. He jumped to his window and peered out, then walked swiftly to his door and threw it open. He almost ran into a younger student in his doorway.

"Do you hear that?" asked Geoffrey Bache Smith. The noise of the students was getting louder, now punctuated by the piercing note of a police whistle.

"Of course! I was just coming to get you. Let's go."

The two young men ran out of their hall and into the street with hundreds of other students joining in the fun. Some were carrying their academic gowns, and some were wearing them open so that they flowed out behind them as they ran. The police employed by the proctors—or "bulldogs," as these university law enforcement agents were called—tried to intervene, but the students simply evaded them.

Running and hooting down the streets, Smith and Tolkien found a motorized bus parked by the road. The city of Oxford had only recently replaced horse-drawn trams with these vehicles. This one was empty. Perhaps the driver had given up trying to navigate streets filled with screaming students and was waiting somewhere for order to return.

"Quick, GB!" yelled Tolkien. He darted into the bus and closed the door as soon as his companion joined him. With a rumble they pulled out into the street and Tolkien accelerated, all the while honking wildly and clanging the bell. Both boys yelled out the windows as well. Soon masses of students and nonstudents were following them on foot, cheering them on. Tolkien began stopping and letting underclassmen get on. He wrote later that "it was chock full of undergrads before it reached the Carfax. There I addressed a few stirring words to a huge mob before descending and removing to the . . . Martyr's Memorial where I addressed the crowd again. There were no disciplinary consequences of all this!"[2]

Tolkien's authorized biographer, Humphrey Carpenter, insists that this was "not untypical" of how Tolkien would entertain himself in the evenings.[3] The craziness of student behavior during "town versus gown rags" was part of the Oxford tradition at that time. Tolkien went to Exeter College in Oxford, a school that would have mostly attracted more serious students, not the wealthy boys who really had no need to do well and would be the leaders of the student "rags" in Oxford. Tolkien, however, readily participated in such activities despite his different circumstances.

Exeter was also a place where Tolkien did not experience as much of the snobbery that he would have if he had gone to a college with more students from the upper class.[4] Even so, Tolkien's experience in pre–World War I Oxford society involved a culture of social distinctions. Oxford was originally for the ruling class in British society. It was a realm that Tolkien had only broken into through a scholarship program. As a student, he got a dorm room (or rather, a sitting room and a tiny bedroom)[5] and the college provided a "scout" for the floor, who was essentially a servant to the students who roomed there. Among other services, the scout would bring Tolkien his breakfast every morning.[6]

The class-consciousness that Tolkien took for granted in his early life is a part of Middle-earth most unfamiliar to more modern readers. There is some evidence that Tolkien himself was ambivalent about the society in which he had been reared. He wrote once that Sam Gamgee, servant in the servant-master relationship with Frodo in the *Lord of the Rings* trilogy, was based on the kind of person whom he "recognized as so far superior to myself."[7]

Tolkien said both positive and negative things about what Sam Gamgee represents, so there is no question that Frodo considered him a true friend. But the discrepancy shows the tension that a more structured world faced in valuing members of society and yet feeling pride or superiority in one's own class.

> The impression of greater age in Sam as compared with Frodo that you feel is due to the representation in these two persons of two quite different characters, each with a quite different background and education. Sam in part of his more complex character retains the sententiousness, and indeed cocksureness, of the rustic of limited outlook and knowledge. He was the youngest son of a stupid and conceited old peasant. Together with his loyal master-servant attitude, and his personal love for Frodo, he retains a touch of the contempt of his kind (moderated to tolerant pity) for motives above their reach. From this in some degree comes his slightly paternal, not to say patronizing attitude to his master; but of course it is mainly derived from the fact that after the encounter by Weathertop Frodo was a sufferer, a person injured and in pain, and also after Rivendell grievously burdened. Sam's protective and almost elderly manner was largely forced on him by circumstance.[8]

The discrepancy may also reflect another kind of tension that Tolkien faced in his early life. He was not exactly one or the other of the two roles represented in Frodo and Sam. Biographer

Humphrey Carpenter portrays both sides of Tolkien's family as commonly engaged in telling stories about ancestors who were said to be in the nobility—which may have reflected on the anxiety felt by struggling members of the British middle class. It is no accident that Tolkien wrote an epic fantasy where royal status was assigned by birth. This was not just a fantasy but his actual politics. "Touching your cap to the Squire may be . . . bad for the Squire but it's . . . good for you."[9] Tolkien displayed this attitude again when he mentioned the era of Jane Austen in a letter to his son Christopher and regretted the vanishing manners. "Little is left of it all, save a few remnants of table manners (among a decreasing minority)," he wrote. "But actually they made life a lot easier, smoother, and less frictional and dubious." Manners did this because they "cloaked or indeed held in check (as table-manners do) the everlasting cat, wolf, and dog that lurk at no great depth under our social skin."[10]

As one trying to establish an academic career, Tolkien had struggles that were almost overwhelming to him. With his aptitude for language and his obvious academic giftedness, one would expect Tolkien to excel in college. But it was not that easy for him. The same problems that hurt him in trying to prepare for and do well in his exams for Oxford also entangled him once he arrived at Oxford. Tolkien was bored. He had been accepted into the Classics program and was thus expected to excel among many students who had all been steeped in Latin and Greek literature. While Tolkien knew such literature and could read it in the original language, he was bored with such curriculum. He wanted to learn more northern European languages and read

Germanic literature. It did not help that Exeter College did not have a Classics tutor in residence for students during Tolkien's first two terms.

After discovering in the Exeter College library a grammar for Finnish, Tolkien devoted time to learning the language so he could read the *Kalevala*. He later wrote, "I never learned Finnish well enough to do more than plod through a bit of the original."[11] Yet, he gave a great deal of time and energy to it rather than to his assigned studies, also using the grammar to work more on private languages. Welsh was another hobby that fascinated him but distracted him from his Classics curriculum.

Tolkien also spent time in student groups with friends. By today's standards, many of his social activities were rigorously academic. While he participated in rugby, he also joined the Essay Club, the Dialectical Society, and the Stapeldon, the debating society at Oxford.[12] He also tried to start clubs of his own, just as he had started the T.C.B.S. at King Edward's. And while Tolkien showed a great deal of energy and intelligence in his recreational activities, not all his diversions were sanctioned by the school. Tolkien engaged in student pranks, including his joy ride on the bus.[13]

Amid all his schoolwork, there was one course that especially interested Tolkien. He had the privilege of taking comparative philology taught by Joseph Wright. Wright was not only a world-class philologist, but he was someone to whom Tolkien had felt especially connected since he had discovered and studied Wright's *Primer of the Gothic Language* back in Birmingham when he was supposed to be studying to get into Oxford.[14] Wright provided him with interesting teaching and with inspiration and personal encouragement.

Despite the distance and the many local activities, Tolkien continued to keep up with his relationships in the T.C.B.S. It had continued without him at King Edward's, involving his younger friends as well as new members. But of those his own age, Christopher Wiseman and Robert Quilter Gilson both went to Cambridge, the former on a mathematics scholarship at Peterhouse and the latter at Trinity, where he studied Classics.[15]

## TWENTY-ONE AT LAST, BUT STILL WAITING

While Tolkien's life had been taken up with a masculine world of academia and sports, he had tenaciously held on to the idea of reuniting with Edith Bratt and proposing marriage to her. So as soon as he turned twenty-one, he immediately wrote her a letter proposing marriage. That was on January 3. On January 8, he traveled in person to where she lived in Cheltenham to persuade her to accept his proposal. This was more difficult than he had expected because she had written back that she was engaged to another man.[16] Nevertheless, he prevailed upon her to remember their past promises to one another and to assure her that though the silence of almost three years had raised doubts, he had never forgotten her and still loved her. She broke off her engagement and agreed to marry Tolkien.

This outcome made Tolkien very happy, but it also put

Edith in a kind of limbo. Even though they were now able to see each other, Tolkien still had a long way to go before he could claim to be a real provider for a family. It was still quite possible that he could fail to win a position that would support Edith and any children they might have. Thus, he did not feel they could announce their engagement publicly right away. He was also fearful of informing Father Morgan. Even though Tolkien had obeyed and was no longer under a guardian's authority, he was still financially dependent on Father Morgan and wanted his blessing. He worried about how the priest would react. In the end, while not happy about Tolkien's return to Edith, Father Morgan did not allow the prospect to weaken his commitment to helping Tolkien during his stay in Oxford.

Tolkien's engagement to Edith would present other challenges, but he first had to worry about upcoming tests. These were officially named "Honour Moderations," but were simply referred to as "mods." They involved writing papers on his subjects. They were graded in "classes" with the highest grade being First Class and the lowest being Fourth Class.[17] A great deal depended on these tests for Tolkien. If he wanted to win an academic position in order to have a source of income so he could marry Edith, he needed to do well. But his months of neglect and now his time spent with Edith made it extremely difficult for him to do as well as many believed he should.

His Classics tutor, Lewis Farnell, was a man dedicated to ancient Greece to the point of being an adventurer and going to Greece himself to visit ancient sites of interest despite the danger of bandits.[18] Despite his tutor's zeal, Tolkien simply did not get excited about the literature or civilization of Homer's world and wrote later that no one could understand "why my essays on the Greek drama were getting worse and worse."[19]

Thus, in taking his mods, Tolkien did not do well for one who hoped to be a professor. Instead of getting a First Class, he got a Second Class, and even that was close. Most of Tolkien's papers only rated a Third Class, except that he turned in an outstanding paper on Greek philology.[20] This was obviously a subject that Tolkien cared about keenly and for which he had a natural aptitude as well. He did so well that it significantly helped his average grade.

Rather than regard Tolkien as second rate or berating him to do better, Farnell gave thought to what would serve Tolkien best and also allow Tolkien to best serve academia. While Farnell possessed a passion for Greek, he also held the northern European languages in high regard. He knew of Tolkien's interest in Germanic languages and suggested to Tolkien that he switch from Classics to English—a course of study that would include older versions of English and other languages that contributed to English, as well as philology. Farnell's help did not stop there. Tolkien's scholarship was for Classics. Using his position as rector of Exeter College,[21] Farnell worked behind the scenes to ensure that Tolkien got to keep his school income even though he was now switching to a different subject.[22] This change in course of study altered Tolkien's life, giving him a new chance to prove himself and making a teaching career possible if he did well in his studies. Tolkien did quite well at taking advantage of this new opportunity.

Once the tests were behind him, he was also able to deal with other issues involved in getting married. One complication in Tolkien's engagement to Edith was her Protestantism. Tolkien wanted and expected Edith to convert to the Roman Catholic Church; he believed husband and wife needed to be members of the same Christian communion. Edith, for her part, did not claim to have any personal theological convictions that prevented her from doing so, and she was quite willing to join. But as an active churchgoing Christian, she was heavily involved in a local Anglican Church. It was an important social circle for her. Also, Edith had a landlord who, she knew, would heartily oppose and be outraged by her conversion to Roman Catholicism.

Tolkien held the ideal of his martyred mother, who had been willing to face a great deal of hostility to become a member of the Roman Catholic Church, and he believed that Edith should show the same resolve and commitment—and be willing to face the same sacrifices. He wrote to her, "I do so dearly believe that no half-heartedness and no worldly fear must turn us aside from following the light unflinchingly."[23] However, it was somewhat problematic for Tolkien to be writing such exhortations since he had allowed his attendance at Mass to lapse in the previous year.[24] As one writer speculates, "It is at least possible that had Tolkien been a better Catholic in 1913, Edith may have been a better Catholic in the years that followed."[25]

Nevertheless, Edith promised to convert and Tolkien held her to it, even though it meant leaving a church where she had friends and moving to a church of strangers. She asked if she could put off this move until they could announce the engagement officially and the time was closer when they would be married, but Tolkien did not want her to delay. Sure enough, when she told her landlord that she intended to become Roman Catholic, he turned her out of his house. She had to find new lodgings with an older cousin. They ended up renting a residence in Warwick.

While there was some initial joy in attending church together, for the most part Edith found herself very much alone. She was never able to find fellowship in the Catholic church in Warwick that came close to what she had at her Anglican parish. She officially became Roman Catholic on January 8, 1914, the one-year anniversary date of her reunion with Tolkien.[26] Despite a happy beginning, Edith began slipping in her attendance and ended up becoming tepid in her commitment. It is likely that Tolkien's pushing her to hurry up and convert may have inspired bad feelings. "The residue of resentment, the result of her being rushed into a decision before she was ready," wrote Joseph Pearce, "remained with Edith for many years, possibly for the remainder of her days."[27]

From his early fiction writings, Tolkien provides evidence that he may have sensed something of the cost that Edith paid. Tolkien related his courtship and marriage of Edith to a story he wrote of an immortal elven maiden, Luthien, sacrificing her immortality in order to marry a mortal man, Beren. This story was eventually published as part of *The Silmarillion*. Tolkien self-consciously equated Luthien with Edith and himself with Beren based on a walk they took in a wood sometime later when Tolkien was recuperating during World War I. He even had

"Luthien" inscribed on Edith's tombstone and "Beren" carved into his own.[28] (A similar love story is found in *The Lord of the Rings* in the courtship of Aragorn and Arwen.)

All this sounds very romantic, and there is no doubt that Tolkien intended it to be. But it also reflects tension that abounded in their marriage. While Edith was glad to be married, she, like Luthien, had to make sacrifices. In addition to the tension over Roman Catholicism, Edith was very much in a separate world from Tolkien's work and teaching, the things about which he felt most passionate. She found herself very much alone, living in academic settings where she had very little interest or background. Tolkien may have exacerbated this separation by his "self-chosen role of sentimental lover."[29] This was not a role that could be meshed with his professional life or his male friends who were so important to him. It entailed keeping Edith separated from the major part of his life.

In the year leading up to Edith's entry into the Roman Catholic Church, Tolkien kept up his friendships by correspondence and through meetings without even mentioning her existence to his close male friends. It was not until autumn 1913, when she would soon become Roman Catholic and their engagement would be formalized, that he wrote to them the news that he was going to get married eventually. When he wrote to them, he even left out the name of his fiancée.[30] In the meantime, Edith, for her part alone in a new place, found it upsetting to receive letters from him full of accounts of "his life of dinner parties and movie-going, college clubs and debating, and tennis and punting."[31]

## THE COUNCIL OF LONDON

Tolkien had maintained friendships from the T.C.B.S. group at King Edward's. With Wiseman and Gilson at Cambridge, however, he had no regular contact with the group. That changed when Geoffrey Smith came in the fall of 1913 to study history at Corpus Christi College in Oxford and also to read English.[32] The two renewed their friendship and stayed in touch even when the war separated them.

Despite Tolkien's diversions at college, his change in direction produced results. In the spring of 1914, he won the Skeat Prize in English,[33] which brought him some award money. He used some of his winnings to purchase some books on medieval Welsh and other books written by William Morris. He purchased *The Life and Death of Jason*, a poem about Jason and the Argonauts that was also beautifully illustrated by Morris. He bought the *Volsunga Saga*, Morris's translation of the legendary saga that had been written in prose in Icelandic in the thirteenth century, and Morris's *The House of the Wolfings and All the Kindreds of the Mark*. This work, featuring a Germanic tribe resisting Roman soldiers, was arguably one of the earliest modern fantasy novels, featuring a forest known as Mirkwood and a war duke named Thiodolf—which is quite close to Theoden, a king in Tolkien's novels.

In December 1914, key members of the T.C.B.S. met at a meeting, which they dubbed the "Council of London." The young men had a habit of naming their meetings as if they were councils of war. In part this was youthful bravado but also probably reflected the onset of World War I. The four of them—Tolkien, Christopher Wiseman, Robert Gilson, and Geoffrey Smith—met in Wiseman's home. There they decided to regard themselves as the real T.C.B.S. and no longer accepted the expanded group, which they felt was not really dedicated to the artistic ideals they wished to promote and embody. While the four certainly loved humor and fun, they felt the others were not serious enough at times.

The four felt they would leave their mark on the world, if only they could survive. Two of the four, Wiseman and Smith, had already joined Britain's armed forces.[34]

Tolkien regarded that meeting as a new chapter in his attempts at creative work. A year and a half later, he credited the Council of London as the turning point when he became aware of "the hope and ambitions (inchoate and cloudy I know)"[35] that motivated him to make new literary achievements. In addition to renewing his development of new languages, he began seriously striving to produce poetry after that initial reunion of the core T.C.B.S.

Some of those poetic fragments survived to be reborn as portions of *The Lord of the Rings*. For example, Tolkien wrote a nonsense poem that expanded on the English nursery rhyme that begins, "Hey diddle diddle, the Cat and the Fiddle . . ."[36] It was the song that Frodo sang at the inn at Bree before he fell and accidentally slipped on the Ring.

Tolkien also took a prose work he had been trying to develop from a portion of the Finnish *Kalevala* that he loved so much and decided to write it as an English epic poem.

While other T.C.B.S. members did not like the comparison, Tolkien saw the group as a new kind of Pre-Raphaelite Brotherhood, a group of literary and visual artists (which, interestingly, had included William Morris). That group had promoted a brand of medievalism as opposed to the more modern trends. As he perceived their vision, he now had a mandate to express "all kind of pent up things"[37] in a way he had not done before.

The vision of the T.C.B.S. was anti-secular and yet non-moralistic. To take one example, when Wiseman, Smith, and Gilson once met at a time Tolkien could not be with them, they complained together about how George Bernard Shaw and Henrik Ibsen had ended Victorian moralism in drama but left a vacuum.[38] Ibsen had produced what were considered scandalous plays because they showed how immorality could and did sow destruction in respectable households. Shaw was influenced by Ibsen and wrote plays of social criticism.

The T.C.B.S. saw themselves as a response to such artistic trends. They would produce creative works that would "re-establish sanity, cleanliness, and the love of real and true beauty in everyone's breast," according to G. B. Smith.[39] Yet, as biographer John Garth has written, "despite the crusading language, the TCBSian cultural and moral manifesto did not involve telling people what to do."[40] This would be a lifelong commitment on the part of Tolkien, one that eventually brought him to change his mind about George Macdonald, whom he loved as a child, and decide that he was but an "old grandmother" who delivered sermons rather than stories.[41]

The T.C.B.S. moral vision was to invite the world to a meal instead of preaching at them.

But who would deliver this invitation to a better world? What Tolkien didn't know is that he would become virtually the sole heir of the T.C.B.S. If they were to have influence on the world, it would have to come through him.

# THE COMING OF THE SHADOW (1915–1918)

Tolkien was never famous as a young man; he was not known to the world until his later years. Not only was his youth a distant memory, but so was the time in which he reached adulthood. An entirely new world war had been fought and was already receding in memory. Yet, for many years of Tolkien's life, he was accustomed to referring to World War I as the "Great War." It was always the Great War of his life—the shadow under which he came of age.

## THE SHADOW OF THE GREAT WAR

While Tolkien's readers might associate the epic tale of the war of the Ring with the struggles that occurred in the second world war, Tolkien insisted it wasn't so and even added a preface to *The Fellowship of the Ring* to persuade readers not to read his work as any kind of commentary on World War II. He insisted also that his trilogy was not allegorical or topical and that it was wrong to look into his intentions for any inner meaning or message. He pointed out that the most decisive chapter setting up the story was written long before 1939, and the unfolding of the war of the Ring bears no resemblance to the unfolding of World War II.

However, in the very preface that claims that the work must not be read as topical, Tolkien points readers to the topic of World War I. "One has indeed personally to come under the shadow of war to feel fully its oppression," he wrote, "but as the years go by it seems now often forgotten that to be caught in youth in 1914 was no less hideous an experience than to be involved in 1939 and the following years." And then, in the middle of the paragraph, before going on to another example, as if he were mentioning nothing that important, he wrote that by 1918 all but one of his close friends were dead.

World War I began with the incident on June 28, 1914, when Archduke Franz Ferdinand of Austria, the heir to the Austro-Hungarian throne, was assassinated in Sarajevo, Bosnia. In response, Austria attacked Serbia. Russia supported Serbia and Germany supported Austria, so Germany declared war on Russia on August 1. In waging this war, Germany invaded France after going through Belgium. Britain demanded that Germany withdraw, but to no avail. Britain declared war on Germany on August 4, 1914. By the end of that year, "nearly the entire British Expeditionary Force of 160,000 men sent to France had been killed."[1]

As the war continued, Tolkien himself delayed entrance into military service until 1915. Some have wondered about this delay: if Tolkien's German ancestry may have made him hesitant to join in the fight or if his love for German culture may have motivated him against joining. For example, at a time when many were changing their German family names into Anglicized names, Tolkien kept his and refused to be ashamed of it.[2] Tolkien also shared respect of German scholarship with his professor and adviser, the philologist Joseph Wright, who attempted to set up a lending library for wounded German prisoners who were being cared for in Oxford.[3]

Another reason proposed for his delayed entrance was a personal sentiment against the war. However, Tolkien and his friends in the T.C.B.S. hoped that their group would be strengthened and fortified through the trials involved in the war. Gilson, while he thought the war was horrible for the world, wrote that the T.C.B.S. might someday "thank God for this war."[4] It was a chance for those in combat to become real heroes. Wiseman wrote that the war might prepare them for a "great work that is to come"—though he didn't yet know what that might be.[5] These sentiments were shared by Tolkien.

Instead, Tolkien had a very practical reason not to volunteer right away. He was in a relatively unique situation at Oxford. Unlike his friends, Tolkien had no economic means to support himself, let alone a family, unless he gained a profession. As his fellow T.C.B.S. member R. Q. Gilson wrote to his girlfriend, Tolkien "has always been desperately poor."[6] He rightly believed his duty to his fiancée entailed that he could not fulfill his duty to England right away. He was aiming at an academic career and could not afford to lose that opportunity. Going to war early would have thrown his entire future, and Edith's, into doubt.

So Tolkien threw himself into his studies, though he continued to also write poetry and use his ability with languages to continue the construction of new ones. In June 1915, Tolkien took his school's exams and this time gained a Full Class Honours degree, thus assuring himself an academic position when he could pursue it after the war. His prospects were secure and now his main challenge was to join in and survive combat duty.

## INTO BATTLE

With the passing of his exams, the deferral of Tolkien's commission came to an end. He was now a second lieutenant in the Lancashire Fusiliers. Geoffrey Smith belonged to the Lancashire Fusiliers, and Tolkien hoped they would be able to serve together. But he was put in the nineteenth battalion, and Smith was a member of the thirteenth.

Tolkien began his arduous military training in Bedford. Here he was able to visit Edith on weekends and shared in the purchase of a motorcycle with another officer so that he could make the trip to Warwick. But in August he was moved to Staffordshire, where he underwent a much rougher life designed to prepare him for what he would face in war.

The following November he wrote Edith a letter that gives a taste of his perception of his military exercises. He described life at Camp Rugeley as one of freezing with occasional bouts of exercise to warm up and then again standing still "in icy groups in the open being talked at!" This was an ironic practice for winter, he observed, because in the summer "we doubled about at full speed and perspiration."[7] British culture demanded some form of tea time even in the midst of training. Tolkien describes fighting to get near a stove just to get a bit of warmth during this break. He also used the heat to put a slice of bread on the end of a knife and toast it.

Like military basic training in almost any time or culture, Tolkien's preparation for combat duty in Europe was grueling. Yet, even in the midst of the continual, exhausting exercises, he continued to work on his artistic ambitions. He told Edith that he had made a pencil copy of a typewritten draft of a poem, "Kortirion" (full title: "Kortirion Among the Trees").

Tolkien continued to work on poetry under harsh conditions and shared the work with the men from the T.C.B.S., despite all the practical difficulties. At that time, even a relatively simple task such as sharing a poem with more than one person entailed recopying it for each recipient or else making arrangements for the recipient to send it on to another person. While the T.C.B.S. sometimes passed on messages to one member on behalf of another to improve their efficiency, Tolkien did not seem to feel comfortable using Edith in this method. In the case of one letter that we have, while writing under time constraints that made it difficult to write long letters, Tolkien took time in his note to show her his mental wavering. He wanted to send the letter to Smith, Wiseman, and Gilson and said, at first, that he would mail them the pencil copy—presumably as a circular to be sent from one of the three men to the next until all had seen it. He promised to Edith that he would send "a careful ink copy for little you," the next night. But then, as he wrote to her, he changed his mind and said he would send the pencil copy to her, assuring her (or himself) that it was neat enough. He said he would wait to make a copy for the T.C.B.S. later, despite feeling he owed all of them long letters.[8] Tolkien's drive to create and his thirst for literary fellowship were increasing in the bleak surroundings of training. He also dealt with tension in trying to include Edith—both acknowledging the importance of the T.C.B.S. and yet sharing his work with Edith as well.

Tolkien chose as his specialty to be a signals officer. While one would think that Tolkien's interest in languages might entail an aptitude for codes, his military test grades were average.[9] His training included sending messages by using a pair of handheld flags and communicating in Morse code by either a transmitter, blinking spotlights, or mirrors reflecting sunlight. He was also taught how to handle field telephones and even carrier pigeons.[10]

As he approached the end of his training, but before he left for France, Tolkien and Edith were married. There was no other way to really provide for his fiancée. If he had further delayed the wedding and was killed in battle, he would leave Edith without any support and worse off than before she had become engaged to him. He needed to ensure that, were he to die, she would gain what little inheritance he had to his name.

Marrying Edith entailed a dreaded meeting with Father

Morgan to enlist his help despite the priest's past opposition to their relationship. Even though Tolkien had turned twenty-one and was no longer under his legal guardianship, Father Morgan was still the possessor of Tolkien's small inheritance. Tolkien needed to get the priest to officially transfer it into his name so that, should he die, Edith would receive it as his widow. Tolkien went to the Oratory in Birmingham and had no real problem making the financial arrangements. But he had intended to also inform Father Morgan that he was now finally getting married to Edith. Once face-to-face with him, he was too intimidated to do so. He ended up waiting until nearly two weeks before the wedding to write and tell him about it. Father Morgan wrote back, kindly giving his blessing to the marriage, offering to officiate, and inviting the couple to use the Oratory church. But by this time arrangements had already been made.

Tolkien and Edith were married March 22, 1916. The ceremony took place in Warwick and was followed by a week's honeymoon in Clevedon, Somerset.[11] Soon after their return to Warwick, Tolkien had to leave for more training.

As before, when she had been waiting for him to finish his studies at Oxford, Edith yet again had to wait and work around his training. Since Tolkien was now about to move as he was commanded, Edith would relocate as necessary and with her cousin find residences close to wherever Tolkien was stationed. Their first move was to Great Haywood in Staffordshire.[12]

On June 2, 1916, Tolkien received his orders to get ready for transport to the north of France across the English Channel. On his final leave before his departure, Tolkien had every reason to fear he would die and never see his wife again—the death rate for junior officers like himself was quite high. They spent a weekend together in Birmingham at a hotel until he departed Sunday evening. He later said that leaving Edith for war was "like a death."[13] He arrived in France on June 6. He was transported to Étaples, where he was forced to wait and do nothing for three weeks. The Allies were planning a major push just to the south in the region of Somme, a territory that adjoined the English Channel.

Tolkien had not thought highly of his training in war, saying that time was wasted on "wearily going over, over, and over again, the dreary topics, the dull backwaters of the art of killing."[14] Now he was in the company of veteran officers who had seen action in the Boer War. As a young man, Tolkien found the older generation of leaders unimpressive and more interested in proving their superiority to the junior officers of his generation than in being real leaders. He later recalled that it was at this time he came to grasp the basis for the character of Sam Gamgee. While the veteran officers did not impress him at all, the noncommissioned officers and the privates who came from a lower social class impressed him very much, although he was not permitted to be friends with them the way he portrayed Frodo's friendship with Sam. While the era of World War I is considered part of the modern age, much of the aristocratic mind-set of the medieval age was still practiced. In the military these social rules were enforced as a matter of regulation. Nevertheless, Tolkien thought these men, who were assigned to help him in various ways, showed themselves worthy of respect and admiration.[15] These men from the working and lower middle classes were likely closest to what would have been Tolkien's own social position if he had not excelled and succeeded in academics—and were likely the same class as his brother, Hilary, who had left farming to become a bugler.[16]

After enduring three weeks of inaction, Tolkien moved with his battalion to the Somme on June 27. The Battle of the Somme began on July 1, 1916, and did not end until November 13, 1916, though Tolkien's Fusiliers were not used in the initial charge. The leadership believed the attack, a major offensive in a northern area of France that straddled from Belgium to the English Channel, would break the stalemate at Verdun to the east near the Belgian border where the French tenaciously held their ground against a German concerted assault. The hope was that by pushing through at the Somme, the Allied forces could give relief to those troops.

The plan involved bombarding the German line so heavily that there would be little resistance left when the British troops charged. This doctrine of "preliminary bombardments" was not a result of wisdom from war experience; it was an untested hypothesis built on speculation about how new technologies that allowed bombing ought to work. Until World War I, this hypothesis had never been subjected to empirical testing. The Battle of the Somme was a major laboratory, and Tolkien was one of about a hundred thousand guinea pigs.

The doctrine was erroneous. Preliminary bombardments were not able to permanently damage a determined enemy ensconced in deep trenches. The German occupiers at the

Somme had the high ground, and they had been given enough time to dig out extensive trenches and even reinforce them with concrete bunkers.

Despite developments with better explosive shells and artillery guns, the strategy of preliminary bombardment never worked the way it was supposed to during World War I. But at the Battle of the Somme, near the beginning of the war, much more went wrong with the plan. Either because the technology had not yet been perfected or not enough resources were utilized, many of the explosive shells failed to explode at all. To this day, farmers in the area are in danger of finding the shells, some of which may have the ability to explode under the right circumstances.

Beginning June 24, eight days before the planned charge on July 1, the Allies shelled the enemy position continually. Then, when the attack began, the British army lost 58,000 men, dead, wounded, or missing. Part of the reason for the tremendous death toll was the overconfidence in the bombing strategy. The "charging" was done at a slow pace with soldiers weighed down with equipment that lessened their agility. Not expecting a great deal of opposition, many simply strode into the No Man's Land only to be cut down by German guns that were ready and waiting. Despite the horrific losses, the plan was continued for several days. The British did gain some territory at a great cost in lives.

The Battle of the Somme served as the debut of the tank. This was an incredibly slow and clumsy vehicle designed as a way to gain ground in trench warfare. There was nothing really "futuristic" about these vehicles. They were noisy, hot, and full of noxious fumes from the machinery that was placed in the cabin with the drivers or passengers. Nevertheless, they made an impact not only on the war but also in the minds of those who witnessed them on the battlefield. They probably inspired some scenes in the fiction that Tolkien would write soon after the battle.

Tolkien and his Lancashire Fusiliers, held back to be ready for later service, witnessed an endless stream of wounded being brought back on "everything with wheels" that could be commandeered for the purpose.[17] Sunday morning he attended Mass at a portable altar officiated by a chaplain from the Royal Irish Rifles.[18] Later, the danger increased as the German artillery began shelling the area, though the village was not hit.[19]

For a while the battalion was put to use burying the endless stream of corpses flowing from the battlefield and the ineffective field hospitals. Eventually the Lancashire Fusiliers were sent into the trenches. Many of Tolkien's companions died. The battlefield was carnage. Dead bodies and parts of bodies were left strewn on the field and in the trenches where they got half buried. Tolkien found that what had once been cornfields and grassy meadows was now an endless mudflat with the ruined remnants of trees jutting skyward, stripped of leaves and many branches. In the place of healthy vegetation, the fields had been seeded with open-eyed, sightless, dead bodies that had been mutilated by machine guns and explosives. A nasty stench accompanied the nightmarish sights.

Tolkien would later write of the Dead Marshes, which

Frodo and Sam had to pass through, in which they saw the dead faces in the muck of dirty pools. "I saw them: grim faces and evil, and noble faces and sad," says Frodo. "Many faces proud and fair, and weeds in their silver hair. But all foul, all rotting, all dead. A fell light is in them."[20] While he claimed most of the inspiration came from William Morris, he did write in a letter that "perhaps in landscape" the scene "owed something to northern France after the Battle of Somme."[21]

Tolkien spent more than three and a half months in the war zone, much in the trenches. He kept in contact with Christopher Wiseman by brief letters. He and G. B. Smith also kept in touch with each other when they could to encourage one another. At one point, however, Smith's letter reported horrible news. Smith had found a list of the dead and the name of R. Q. Gilson was present. He had been killed on the first day of the campaign with the tens of thousands of other soldiers who died. This loss, amid all the other deaths he witnessed and heard about, affected Tolkien deeply, and he wondered what to think of the ambitions that had so excited the T.C.B.S. in peacetime. His companions consoled him, however, and he even got to meet up with G. B. Smith in the village of Bouzincourt. During their supper together the village was fired upon.[22]

Tolkien was spared from wounds of battle. But there were other risks in the midst of war besides the actual fighting. The exposed corpses scattered around the battlefields attracted rats and other vermin. Those vermin carried disease and insects that carried disease. One of the things they carried was lice.

Troops holding the trenches, especially trenches that had

been taken from the Germans, had to deal with armies of lice that would burrow into all the soldiers' clothes in every crease and pocket where they could hide. Body lice spread among soldiers crowded together in trenches. Anecdotal evidence comes from the Anglican chaplain to the Lancashire Fusiliers, Rev. Mervyn S. Evers, who wrote in his memoirs about himself and some companions, one of whom may have been J. R. R. Tolkien, "the Signals Officer." They were in a trench captured from the Germans and tried to get to sleep but could not because of "hordes" of attacking lice. They found the medical officer and acquired from him an ointment he promised would "keep the little brutes away." The soldiers followed his orders dutifully by covering themselves in the ointment and then again tried to get some sleep. But it was not possible. The medicine, "instead of discouraging them," Evers wrote, "seemed to act like a kind of hors d'oeuvre and the little beggars went at their feast with renewed vigour."[23]

Lice carried the bacteria *Rickettsia quintana* (also called *Bartonella quintana*) that caused the illness known as "trench fever." Their bites spread the germs into the bloodstream, and while the resulting sickness was not typically fatal, it was long lasting and debilitating. Also called "five-day fever," the disease causes continual relapsing. After a two-week incubation period, sufferers experienced the sudden onset of a fever and severe headaches. The disease showed symptoms differently in various patients. Some recovered after an initial few days of sickness. Others had relapses every five days for several episodes that gradually became less severe. But Tolkien was in a third group, who had symptoms that linger on and off for months (and in some cases years).

Tolkien was pulled from the front on October 27, 1916. After spending days in a hospital at Le Touquet, he was shipped back to England on November 8. His fever would not go away. A train took him to Birmingham and the hospital there. Not until December was he well enough to be released. He was not considered healthy enough to be put back in the combat zone but was permitted leave to visit Edith in Great Haywood. There, in a letter from Christopher Wiseman, he received some more bad news. Another member of the T.C.B.S. was dead. Geoffrey Bache Smith had been killed even though he was not in a battle at the time. As he walked down a village road behind the battle lines, a shell exploded nearby, and shrapnel cut into his right arm and thigh. He died from gas gangrene in his wounds on December 3, 1916.[24] After describing what happened, Wiseman concluded his short note with a prayer that he would be "accounted worthy"[25] of his friend who had been killed.

Before any of them had died, Smith had written to Tolkien about the aspirations of the group and asked him to pass on his sentiments to Wiseman, promising to do the same in a letter to Gilson. He wanted Tolkien to be confident that, though death could destroy individuals, death could not dissolve the group. Smith said his "chief consolation," knowing that he might die, was that there would be someone else to survive "to voice what I dreamed and what we agreed upon." He prayed God's blessing on Tolkien if he should be the one to survive and "say the things I have tried to say long after I am not there to say them."[26]

Smith had written the perfect antidote to Tolkien's despair about the loss of members of the group. Tolkien had written Smith, after hearing that Gilson had been killed, that he felt that the T.C.B.S. was gone: "I do not feel I am a member of a complete body now."[27] But Smith disagreed. His letter had articulated a more positive interpretation. If Tolkien felt as if part of his body had died with the death of a T.C.B.S. member, then it would also be true that the T.C.B.S. member still lived as long as another member survived. Thus there was still a chance for the goals of the group to be fulfilled even if only one member was left to fulfill them.

## IN THE AFTERMATH

As someone who had lost both parents, Tolkien had found a new family in his school friends of the T.C.B.S. In them he found fun and camaraderie in sports, as well as in academic and artistic pursuits and hobbies such as literature, poetry, creative writing, drama, history, and the creation of new languages. Both as friends who spent time with him and then also as correspondents, they were his companions in his teens and early twenties. Vincent Trought had died before World War I started. Robert Q. Gilson had died in the first day of the Battle of the Somme. G. B. Smith, a later member of the inner circle of the T.C.B.S., had been killed by shrapnel. A sometime member, Ralph Payton, had also been killed. Of the original T.C.B.S., only Tolkien and Christopher Wiseman survived.

Tolkien also knew of many more friends, fellow students,

and relatives who died during World War I, in addition to the many soldiers with whom he served who died or were wounded. What was true of the T.C.B.S. could also be said of that entire generation that was decimated during the Great War. According to Garth's *Tolkien and the Great War*, for every eight men who were mobilized to fight, one was killed.[28] But for those in the social class in which Tolkien strove to succeed, the leadership class who attended England's schools like King Edward's, the death rate was much higher, closer to one death in five.[29]

In the midst of this epic slaughter that affected all the European powers came a revolution in world politics. When Tolkien wrote of kings and kingdoms, he was writing substantially about the political world in which he was born but which had ended on the battlefield when he was a young adult. The economist Hans-Herman Hoppe points out that before World War I there were only three constitutional republics (and Portugal had only become one in 1911). Britain, despite being a monarchy, vested ultimate political power in parliament, but it was the only European kingdom or empire to do so. Yet, after the war was over, "monarchies all but disappeared, and Europe along with the entire world entered the age of democratic republicanism."[30]

In Europe, the militarily defeated Romanovs, Hohenzollerns, and Hapsburgs had to abdicate or resign, and Russia, Germany, and Austria became democratic republics with universal— male and female—suffrage and parliamentary governments. Likewise, all of the newly created successor states, with the sole exception of Yugoslavia, adopted democratic republican constitutions. In Turkey and Greece, the monarchies were overthrown. And even where monarchies remained nominally in existence, as in Great Britain, Italy, Spain, Belgium, the Netherlands, and the Scandinavian countries, monarchs no longer exercised any governing power. Universal adult suffrage was introduced, and all government power was vested in parliaments and "public" officials.[31]

In a span of very few years, accompanied by massive loss of life and well-being, Tolkien's world was transformed from one dominated by royal dynasties to one where they were virtually extinct. The alteration was as profound as the end of any of the legendary ages that he wrote about in his fiction.

## RECOVERY AND CREATIVITY

It was during this time of cycling between sickness and recovery that Tolkien began to write his own heroic tales. At the time he referred to them as *The Book of Lost Tales*—the title under which they were posthumously published. Tolkien would eventually involve more humans in the tales, rather than otherworldly creatures (in his first work, Beren was despised by an elf lord not because he was a mortal human but because he was a gnome). Intriguingly, in the most complete tale, "The Fall of Gondolin," the enemy invades the city using mechanical fire-powered carriers made of iron—quite likely a reference to the tanks that were first used in the Battle of the Somme, which Tolkien must have witnessed.

While many elements in Tolkien's imaginary world would change in later stories, it was at this time that Tolkien made new developments that remained present when he eventually wrote *The Lord of the Rings*. He had written many poems about fairies, gnomes, or elves as more or less the same sort of small or tiny beings. Now the elves were a larger-than-life superhuman race closer to gods or unfallen humans than to fairies or gnomes. The elves of Norse and Germanic mythology that Tolkien was familiar with had been more like spirits in trees and streams in many cases, but for Tolkien they became a much more physical race, immortal and magical, but still a biological race of beings that could be hurt and even killed. This allowed him to write stories about elves and battles that were directly applicable to human battles—elf heroism could be a model for human heroism. He later wrote that he viewed his elves as "certain aspects of Men and their talents and desires, incarnated in my little world."[32]

Fairies were quite popular in pre–World War I Britain and had even appeared in war propaganda. Perhaps, having lived through it, Tolkien decided that "fairy tales" related to war required a better breed of elf.[33] He later wrote that, while occasional fairies had been of small size, "smallness was not characteristic of that people as a whole."[34]

## THE WAR'S SLOW ENDING

In early 1917, Tolkien was enjoying life with Edith in a way he had not been able to before. His relapses prevented him from returning to the combat zone. Recovering, again he was moved to Yorkshire. Edith and her cousin followed him north. But there he relapsed again and was sent to an infirmary in Harrogate.[35]

Tolkien went through this process several more times. Edith became pregnant and went to Cheltenham to have the baby, John Francis Reuel Tolkien, who was born on November 16, 1917. As Tolkien continued to be moved around between stations and hospitals as he suffered relapses, Edith now had to survive alone while caring for a small child and suffering from the severe problems she had in delivery. In October 1918, Tolkien was released for the last time from a hospital. The war was finally coming to an end—Tolkien had been spared the fate of members of his entire battalion, who all had been killed or captured.

# LANGUAGE AND LEGEND, PART ONE (1918–1925)

**T**olkien was keenly interested in mythology, fairy tales, and languages. But nothing that happened in the first quarter century of his life, nor his giftedness, nor his passion, guaranteed that Tolkien would be able to use these interests to produce anything worth remembering—the T.C.B.S. goal. Despite his artistic ambitions, he had responsibilities to his employers and to his students to be a good teacher, and to his family to be a good provider. Nevertheless, Tolkien persevered, in the midst of all his other work, in writing and rewriting. He had promised friends, including dear friends who had been killed before their time, that he would pursue an artistic endeavor. As one biographer puts it, Tolkien had, from his time recuperating from trench fever, begun to demonstrate he had "the soul of a writer" by his constant use of spare moments from work to do his own writing.[1]

## DICTIONARY WORK AND TUTORING

After the war ended and as his health improved, Tolkien realized he needed to find a way to make a living. He found an entry through his relationship with William Craigie, who had been his undergraduate tutor in Icelandic and was also an editor on the *Oxford English Dictionary*.[2] This was a multivolume work that had taken so long to complete that there was immediate need to write new supplements. He got permission from the army to live at Oxford—ostensibly to complete his education—and was soon working as an assistant lexicographer on the dictionary project, responsible for the words beginning with *w*. He moved his wife, son, and wife's cousin into rented rooms there.

This provided Tolkien with income for work that was within his specialty. Returning soldiers who were again students needed his services, and he made extra money working with them. He also found an outlet for his creative work. At the Essay Club he publicly read his tale of "The Fall of Gondolin."[3]

Though working for the *Oxford English Dictionary* project was not lucrative, Tolkien was able to get enough tutoring work to substantially help his income. He was in particular demand because he was a married man tutoring out of his home, and the female students were able to learn from him without having to arrange for a chaperone.[4] Oxford had two women's colleges, Lady Margaret Hall and Saint Hugh's,[5] which supplied Tolkien with all the students he needed. Tolkien truly had a calling as a teacher and found that he was both passionate about the subject and gifted at the skill of passing on both his knowledge and passion to his students.[6]

That passion for languages meant that, for him, working on the *Oxford English Dictionary* was quite rewarding, and even educational. He said later that he had learned more in those two years working on the dictionary than in any other two years of his life.[7] He was appreciated for his work. Tolkien's overseer, editor-in-chief Dr. Henry Bradley, said that he had never met anyone as young as Tolkien with such a grasp of Anglo-Saxon and "the comparative grammar of the Germanic languages."[8]

With regular work for the dictionary and tutoring, in the summer of 1919, Tolkien rented a bigger house, one that could fit Edith's piano, which had been in storage, and hired a cook-housemaid.[9] They were now expecting their second child. Through hard work, Tolkien was able to support a growing family, and in 1920, his work as a tutor had become substantial enough that he resigned from his position with the *Oxford English Dictionary*.

Because Tolkien was at the bottom of his career ladder, he needed to be attentive to opportunities to advance. Despite having only recently moved into a new residence, when one of his old Oxford tutors told Tolkien about a teaching position at the University of Leeds, Tolkien applied for it. Somewhat to his surprise, he was interviewed and received a job offer for reader in English language, a position above that of tutor—more or less equivalent to an associate professor in the United States.[10]

Thus, in the summer of 1920, Tolkien was once again separated temporarily from his wife, who was quite pregnant and unable to relocate. When the child, Michael Hilary Reuel Tolkien, was born on October 22, 1920, Tolkien was unable to attend the birth.[11] He wasn't able to move his family up to Leeds until late 1921 when he found a small house to rent.

## LIFE AT LEEDS

George Gordon, the professor of English at the University of Leeds, gave Tolkien the task of creating a specialization for the English department for Anglo-Saxon and Middle English, as opposed to the other program that was already established for students to study post-Chaucerian literature. Tolkien was quite effective in this task. Although Tolkien tried to move on from the University of Leeds early in his time there, applying to schools in Liverpool and being offered a job in Cape Town, South Africa,[12] both he and Edith ended up quite happy at Leeds once they were settled there. The students were from a working-class background and tended to be grateful for the opportunity for an education. As Tolkien wrote about the students, they possessed the "primary qualification" for the capacity to be educated, which was the "willingness *to do some work.*"[13] For similar reasons, Edith found it possible to fit into the community at the University of Leeds and was neither intimidated nor overwhelmed by elitist attitudes.

In addition to teaching, Tolkien also worked hard on projects with E. V. Gordon when he came to the university. Originally from British Columbia, Canada, Gordon had much in common with Tolkien as a scholar and lover of philology and

Germanic literature. He had attended Victoria College locally and then moved to McGill University in Montreal, Quebec, to continue his studies. Receiving a Rhodes Scholarship brought him to University College in Oxford in 1920. Tolkien tutored him that year.[14] This relocation also put Leeds University within reach when they had an opening, and he joined the faculty in 1922. Tolkien and Gordon became good friends.

Gordon's major work was to be his *An Introduction to Old Norse*, but that was after Tolkien had moved on from Leeds. Tolkien first recruited Gordon to assist him in *A Middle English Vocabulary*. Tolkien had been working on the project for some time but had been unable to finish the work. One of Tolkien's former tutors had compiled a book of selections of Middle English literature, and Tolkien wanted to produce a glossary to help students read it. Gordon proved to Tolkien to be a productive worker; the *Vocabulary* was published in 1922.

For a subsequent project, Tolkien and Gordon collaborated on an edition of *Sir Gawain and the Green Knight*, an important project since at the time there was no compilation appropriate for college students. Published by Clarendon in 1925, their original-language edition was the academic standard for Anglo-Saxon students for decades after.

At the age of thirty-three, Tolkien decided to apply to be the professor of Anglo-Saxon at Oxford since the position was now being advertised. Tolkien's letter of application, sent on June 27, 1925, is valuable because it shows us what he had accomplished in the previous years.[15] "A chair which affords such opportunity of expressing and communicating an instructed enthusiasm for

Anglo-Saxon studies and for the study of the other Germanic languages is naturally attractive to me," he wrote, "nor could I desire anything better than to be reassociated in this way with the Oxford English School."[16]

Tolkien explained that he had been accepted at the faculty of Leeds to be a reader in English language where he had a "free commission" to work in the School of English Studies to develop its "linguistic side." He grew it from five participating students out of about sixty to a ratio of twenty studying linguistics to forty-three specializing in literature. Tolkien had personally taught courses in Old English heroic verse, third-year Old Icelandic, and Gothic during his time at Leeds. Specifically, in the last year (fall 1924 through spring and summer 1925) he had also taught the history of English, various Old and Middle English texts, the philology of Old English and Middle English, introductory Germanic philology, and medieval Welsh.

It is clear from his letter that Tolkien believed his job extended beyond the official classroom. He mentions that he managed to attract more than fifteen students, not all of them specializing in linguistics, to a voluntary reading course that involved texts not included on the official syllabus. Additionally, his work had resulted in the founding of a Viking Club by students and faculty who had come to love Old Icelandic or Old Norse (two names for the same language). Tolkien's own commitment to Icelandic is what had resulted in more than two years' worth of courses being offered at Leeds (rather than only one). As he wrote in his letter of application to Oxford, Icelandic was covered "in much the same detail as Anglo-Saxon."[17]

The Viking Club, Tolkien mentioned in his letter, had been started with Gordon's help. The two made it into an entertaining and educational cultural experience. They read Icelandic sagas in the original language and taught each other and sang drinking songs in Icelandic—which was only appropriate because they drank beer with the students as well. They also made up some of their own songs and translated other songs into Old English and to Gothic, set to traditional English tunes. These were later compiled as *Songs for the Philologists*—one of the rarest and most valuable Tolkien collectibles.[18] Its existence shows us how Tolkien had some fun with his students while building a sense of pride in them and recruiting others to his linguistic cause. Later, one of Tolkien's contributions to the collection is attributed to Sam Gamgee in chapter 12 of *The Fellowship of the Ring*. It begins, "Troll sat alone on his seat of stone, and munched and mumbled a bare old bone." Originally entitled "The Root and the Boot," a version was renamed "The Stone Troll" in a collection of poems Tolkien published in 1961, *The Adventures of Tom Bombadil*. Though the story recounts an encounter between a stone troll and a character named Tom, it actually originated from before Tolkien had invented Tom Bombadil.[19]

## WRITING EVER ONWARD

It was not all smooth sailing at Leeds. In 1923, Tolkien was seriously ill with pneumonia and recuperated slowly. During this same year, Tolkien approached the ending of *The Book of Lost Tales* that he had been working on since getting sick as a soldier during World War I. But he did not finish it. Instead he began recasting and rewriting the stories he had already completed. In this sense, while Tolkien may have demonstrated "the soul of a writer" in his regular devotion of time to write without reward, he didn't necessarily have the soul of a *successful* writer—at least not one who might be professionally and financially successful.

Why the reluctance to bring his creation to completion? Biographer Leslie Ellen Jones points to the possibility, from an observation made by Christopher Wiseman, that Tolkien avoided ever completing a project because doing so would mean that he was no longer being creative. The act of invention must end when the invention is completed.[20]

Tolkien's first authorized biographer, Humphrey Carpenter, suggests that Tolkien may have decided that his creative work was unpublishable and thus avoided the unpleasant experience of that kind of "failure."[21] But he is not confident of this answer, pointing to the fantasy stories of Lord Dunsany, who had written many stories both before and after World War I. Lord Dunsany had even created a self-complete world with its own history and gods (named "Pegana"), just as Tolkien was doing in the *Lost Tales*. Perhaps Tolkien saw enough difference between himself and Dunsany to doubt whether he represented hope for his own work. Or perhaps Dunsany's level of success was not enough to satisfy Tolkien at that point in his life. To the extent that *The Book of Lost Tales* represented Tolkien's artistic ambitions going back to the T.C.B.S., it may be that even the thought of getting published might have felt like a failure to him since his success would probably not measure up to the artistic revolution envisioned by the young men of the T.C.B.S.

However, providence was preparing Tolkien to be a much greater author than he or the members of the T.C.B.S. could have predicted. Rather than writing a work that would only appeal to the few fantasy readers, Tolkien recruited millions more into that genre and gave it new life. But he did not do this through his invented legends of the creation of the world, "The Fall of Gondolin," or his story of Luthien and Beren. He did it with a much more detailed and accessible story about hobbits. Once he started writing *The Hobbit*, Tolkien's earlier work provided for him a complex history and background in which to set his story and characters. Rather than someone inventing a history quickly for the sake of the story, by the time Tolkien was writing his story, he had "lived" in his imaginary world for decades. He had a thoroughly developed universe in which to tell his story.

## UP FROM LEEDS

In 1924, at age thirty-two, Tolkien was made a full professor—professor of English language—a young age for such a position by the standards of his day. In part he was given the professorship to make up for his not getting promoted to head of the English department when George Gordon left the university earlier.[22] In 1922, Gordon had accepted a position at Oxford. Tolkien believed that he was qualified to be made head of the department and take Gordon's vacant position, but the vice chancellor had promised the university would soon establish another chair in the English department.[23]

Tolkien's full professorship provided not only academic prestige but also better pay so that Tolkien could buy a better house than the one they were renting. This provided space for the third son born to Tolkien and Edith on November 21, 1924, Christopher John Reuel, named after Christopher Wiseman. Wiseman and Tolkien had grown apart in the aftermath of World War I, but they remained committed friends.

By all accounts, life in Leeds treated Tolkien and his family quite well even if it was not as prestigious as an Oxford professorship. As briefly referred to earlier in this text, in 1925 he heard news about William Craigie, the man who had hired him to work on the *Oxford English Dictionary*. Craigie had resigned as Oxford professor of Anglo-Saxon to go to the University of Chicago. Despite his youth and his recent acceptance of a professorship at Leeds, Tolkien applied for the position that Craigie vacated.

There were three other applicants he knew, all of whom were as or more qualified to get the job. One candidate withdrew his application during the process; one of the two other candidates was chosen to become professor of Anglo-Saxon. It looked as though Tolkien was going to stay at Leeds. But that was not the case. The candidate turned down the job offer, leaving the choice between Tolkien and one of his tutors, Kenneth Sisam, who was now working at Oxford's Clarendon Press. Sisam had been the compiler of *Fourteenth Century Verse and Prose*, for which Tolkien, with Gordon, had produced a glossary.

The contest between Sisam and Tolkien was a close one. Though Sisam held no teaching position at the time, his presence at Oxford was more appealing to a certain kind of snobbery that looked down on Leeds.[24] But not all the faculty had this perspective, especially not George Gordon, who had worked with Tolkien and was now at Oxford as professor of English literature. In the end, Gordon made a great difference in the outcome. The vote was split evenly between the two candidates, which meant that the tie had to be broken by the vice chancellor. He was influenced by Gordon and decided to hire Tolkien.[25]

In 1925, Tolkien began to work as an Oxford don, the professor of Anglo-Saxon. As had happened before, he had to leave his family behind until he could find suitable housing. Late in the year, he found a house on Northmoor Road and settled himself, his wife, and his sons there. Though they moved next door in 1929, they did not leave Northmoor Road until 1947.[26]

## FROM MIDGARD TO MIDDLE-EARTH: SAGAS AND NORSE MYTHOLOGY

One of Tolkien's major extra activities at Oxford was the formation of another Viking Club. He named it the *Kolbitar*, or Coalbiters—an Icelandic name for those gathering close to the fire trying to stay warm, so close that they supposedly bit the coal. While his Leeds club was mainly aimed at reaching students, the *Kolbitar* was more of an attempt to reach out to fellow teachers and was made up of Oxford dons. This may have required more patience for Tolkien since these were not men who had taken an Icelandic language class. They were learning it as a hobby and attempting to read a saga in the original language.

Tolkien's passion for Norse "Viking" stories was reflected in his fantasy stories. The Midgard of Norse mythology became "Middle-earth." Tolkien readers who read the short, popular collection of translated sagas published as part of the Oxford World's Classics series will see how vividly Middle-earth jumps off the pages. While in *The Hobbit* one is early introduced to Thorin Oakenshield, in the sagas, one constantly trips over his near kin with names like Thorarin, Thorbrand, Thord, Thorfinn Skull-splitter, Thorgrim, Thorhall, Thorkell, Thorir, Thorvald, Thorsein the Red, and Thorstein Staff-Struck. Among the rest of Bilbo's dwarf companions, Tolkien included the brothers, Dori, Nori, and Ori, all of whom sound like the famous Icelandic character Snorri. One cannot help but think of the hobbit Frodo when one reads of the location of Froda (named for a Danish king). Olaf the White may not be spelled very much like Gandalf the White but it sounds quite similar. The stallion Freyfaxi shows up, reminding anyone who has read Tolkien's trilogy of Shadowfax. Bjorn is a common name reminding one of Beorn the shape-shifter ("skin-changer") in *The Hobbit*.

Because Old Norse is the same language as Icelandic, not all sagas written in Icelandic actually came from that country. One of the sagas that most interested Tolkien was the *Volsunga*, a legendary saga originating in Norway but taking place in

Iceland. Sagas that originated here were as much legal stories as they were adventurous myths. As economist David Friedman has pointed out, disputes in court are as important to the later sagas as battles are, with the hero of the most famous saga "so skilled in law that no one was considered his equal."[27] But the earlier sagas were of a different sort, including the presence of Norse gods and other aspects of Norse mythology. The *Volsunga Saga* was the story of the Volsung clan, and includes the legend of Sigurd slaying the dragon Fafnir, a story that fascinated Tolkien from when he was a boy. In the *Volsunga Saga*, the hero slays a dragon and gets great treasure, a hero repairs a broken sword that he inherited, and an immortal Valkyrie, Brynhild, becomes mortal to marry a mortal man.[28]

The *Kolbitar* included the Oxford professor of comparative philology, G. E. K. Braunholtz, who knew Icelandic. The professor of Byzantine and modern Greek, R. M. Dawkins, was also a member and had some ability in Icelandic.[29] Other members knew little or no Icelandic, including the professor of English literature and the one who had originally hired Tolkien at Leeds, George Gordon. Exeter College's Nevill Coghill was also a member who did not know Icelandic when he joined. One member was to become an important part of Tolkien's life: C. S. Lewis.

# LANGUAGE AND LEGEND, PART TWO (1926–1937)

While Tolkien's *Kolbitar* was not a student group, Tolkien started it, in part, for the sake of Oxford students. In addition to enjoyment and promoting the Icelandic sagas for their own sake, the group was a part of Tolkien's lobbying efforts to alter the curriculum. When Tolkien came to Oxford, he found an English syllabus divided between an emphasis on literature and linguistics. The literature side emphasized Shakespeare and other later canonized works. The linguistic side, which dealt more with the history of the English language, emphasized philological studies without encouraging students to get wide experience in the ancient literature and languages. Each specialty was somewhat stymied by the other because the professors had all continually lobbied for students to take their individual classes. In theory, the curriculum embodied the high-minded principle that graduates would know all aspects of English scholarship. In reality, it may have had more to do with every professor wanting the maximum number of English students.[1]

Tolkien did not believe the results were adequate. He felt that students of philology needed more time to concentrate on their specialty and more exposure to the languages that were related to Old and Middle English. He also felt that those concentrating on literature should not have to necessarily work through philological studies.

## FROM COAL TO INK

To get his way in revising the syllabus, Tolkien needed to convince the Oxford English faculty to agree with him. As a newcomer to the university, it would not be easy. It took six years before he persuaded the faculty to go along with him—"a lightning-strike revision" by the standards of change for Oxford.[2]

One of the major steps in getting Tolkien's changes implemented was turning C. S. Lewis into an advocate. Lewis and Tolkien first met on May 11, 1926, at a faculty meeting for the English department in what appears to have been one of the times that Tolkien advocated changing the syllabus.[3] Lewis wasn't too impressed at the time. He said later that he had been taught by his Protestant family and then his English literature professors never to trust a papist or a philologist.[4] Tolkien was doubly suspect to him.

But Tolkien and Lewis had too many shared loves not

to become friends. Lewis greatly admired Norse mythology, though he had never before attempted to read any of it in Icelandic. Their common literary interest became more and more evident to both of them. It wasn't too long after they first met that Tolkien invited Lewis to join the *Kolbitar*.

In the meantime, as Lewis and Tolkien began their friendship, Edith gave birth to the Tolkiens' last child on June 18, 1929, Priscilla Mary Reuel Tolkien. Tolkien was a regular attender of Mass who made a point of confessing his sins to a priest as preparation. He raised all his children in that faith even though Edith was not as comfortable with the confessional and did not attend church regularly. While she was a Christian, she was not sure how she felt about her decision to become a Roman Catholic in order to marry one.

Despite Tolkien's traditional faith and Lewis's skepticism, they were drawn to one another. Tolkien came to trust Lewis as a friend and fellow artist before Lewis ever committed himself fully to the Christian faith. It was in 1929 that Tolkien gave Lewis his draft of *The Gest of Beren and Luthien* ("gest" or "geste"—pronounced *jest*—is a Middle English word still used sometimes for a "notable adventure or exploit" and for a poetic or prose "romance or tale").[5] Tolkien had first written it during World War I as one of the *Lost Tales*. It told of the love of an elf maiden and a mortal man and their quest (which he associated with himself and Edith). Though Tolkien had first written the story as prose, he had changed it into a poem.

Lewis greatly appreciated the work but made some suggestions about changing it in places. In so doing, he got to experience Tolkien's perfectionism and independence. Tolkien didn't exactly accept many of the suggestions, but he rewrote the whole poem so that it was virtually transformed. As Lewis later said, "His standard of self-criticism was high and the mere suggestion of publication usually set him upon a revision, in the course of which so many new ideas occurred to him that where his friends had hoped for the final text of an old work they actually got the first draft of a new one."[6]

Tolkien's perfectionism was so acute at this point that he never published any of the original research expected of him as an Oxford scholar. He himself had expected to do more of the kind of work he had done in Leeds on *Sir Gawain and the Green Knight* and the Middle English glossary.[7] While time was a factor—he made ends meet for his family by freelancing as an exam grader in addition to a great deal of teaching—without someone to help him the way E. V. Gordon had helped him with *Sir Gawain*, Tolkien never let go. In the end, Tolkien did manage to get a few works into print, and they were well received.

In regard to his "extracurricular" writing, Lewis's gift to Tolkien was help in completing projects. He was an encourager to Tolkien—assuring him that his work was worth doing and that it was important to finish it. In this process, Tolkien passed a kind of character test. He had to accept help and respond to encouragement by actually producing finished work rather than eternally rewriting it.

Tolkien met a more significant challenge in helping his friend fully commit to the Christian faith. Lewis's sticking point in 1931 was that he could not understand the historical claims about Jesus' death and resurrection as holding real significance for the redemption of the human race. To Lewis, it all seemed far too mythical, and though he admitted to the beauty of the pagan myth of the god dying and rising again, he considered the myth to be evidence that the New Testament account could not possibly be true.

He presented his objections to Tolkien and their friend Hugo Dyson, a fellow at Merton College in Oxford.[8] They both responded that just because the myths did not happen literally did not mean that the myths were not significantly true. They represented a truth that needed to be realized in space and time. So it was perfectly possible that Jesus—the real Son of God—could live out a story that resembled the myths but do so in actual history.[9] Lewis forever after considered this discussion a pivotal moment in the process of his conversion to Christianity.

Eventually the *Kolbitar* came to an end when the men had completed their objective of reading the sagas. But Lewis and Tolkien continued to meet and continued to invite other men (and only men) to regular discussions. An undergraduate, Edward Tangye Lean, the editor of the university magazine, *Isis*, had started a group dubbed the Inklings, to provide an opportunity for members to read to one another what they were writing.[10] The membership included professors, and Tolkien read his poem *Errantry* at one of the early meetings.[11]

The Inklings was not a formal group with a members' roster or attendance records like other clubs at Oxford. Still, it became famous after Tolkien dedicated the first two books in the *Lord of the Rings* trilogy to the group. In addition to Lewis and

Tolkien, members included Owen Barfield, Warren "Warnie" Lewis (who was C. S. Lewis's older brother), Hugo Dyson, and several others. Later Tolkien's son Christopher became an attendee, and Lewis brought in the other most famous member of the group, Charles Williams, an author of many books, including works of fiction that were a kind of predecessor to contemporary fantasy books.

## YOU NEVER KNOW WHERE YOUR FEET MAY LEAD YOU

*The Hobbit*, Tolkien's first full published novel, began when the *Kolbitar* group was still reading the sagas, probably in 1931.[12] Tolkien continued to diligently work on his writing of what became known as *The Silmarillion*—the legends and history of the first and second ages of Middle-earth that had evolved from his earlier work *The Book of Lost Tales*. He considered this serious writing, and he shared it with Lewis and others in the Inklings.

One audience for which Tolkien *did* finish his works was his children. He loved and doted on them and, in doing so, wrote them entertaining stories. When his son Michael lost his toy dog, Tolkien wrote about a dog named Rover who got turned into a self-moving toy by the sand-sorcerer Psamathos Psamathides[13]—almost certainly a recall of E. Nesbitt's *The Five Children and It* featuring a "sand-fairy" called a Psammead. He also wrote and illustrated annual "letters from Father Christmas" to his children. Even here sometimes the universe of Middle-earth leaks through, such as when the Goblins attack

Father Christmas's cellar. "Polar Bear was squeezing, squashing, trampling, boxing, and kicking Goblins sky-high, and roaring like a zoo," wrote Father Christmas, "and the Goblins were yelling like engine whistles."[14] The text itself was only a minor part of the attraction. These letters were beautifully handwritten and included extensive illustrations. In describing how Polar Bear fought the Goblins, Father Christmas said that he couldn't describe it but had included the picture. Polar Bear scribbled in the letter that the picture was inaccurate because he had fought a thousand Goblins rather than only fifteen, but Father Christmas said there was no way he could draw a thousand Goblins.

These illustrated letters were produced in time for Christmas from 1925 to 1938. Despite Tolkien's passion for revision and perfecting, his habit of rewriting and rewriting again, he did have the capacity to finish creative works. If he thought the work was "important," he had trouble letting go. But if it was a matter of playing games with children, then he didn't get as self-conscious and paralyzed. He also showed a real aptitude for being whimsical.

The character Tom Bombadil shows that not only did Middle-earth have a habit of intruding on Tolkien's children's fiction, but his more whimsical fiction sometimes invaded Middle-earth. Tom Bombadil was based on a doll that Michael owned. After writing stories about Tom, Tolkien published a poem about him in *Oxford Magazine* in 1934, having no idea how Tom would end up helping some hobbits. Bombadil comes into the story of *The Fellowship of the Ring* as a strange character who seems supernatural even by the standards of that magical realm. Not even Sauron's Ring can affect him. In part, this strangeness may be the result of being a whimsical creation that was only later inserted into a story about Middle-earth.

Hobbits, or Halflings as they were called by some in *The Lord of the Rings*, were unknown by smell to Smaug the Dragon and had remained hidden from the knowledge of most of the powerful. Neither Sauron nor Saruman had thought much about them. The hobbits had no part in *The Silmarillion*, and Tolkien was not trying to add to *The Silmarillion* when he wrote about Bilbo Baggins. But as the world of Middle-earth broke into the story, it became a tale of Bilbo walking into the world of Tolkien's legendary history. The hobbits being relatively unknown to the wise or to men is appropriate. They are the observers of the world and, despite being hobbits rather than men, often stand in for the reader, asking the right questions to be guided through Middle-earth.

Thus, while Tolkien eventually wrote a story in which hobbits—to the amazement of everyone—saved Middle-earth, they also amazingly saved Middle-earth from obscurity in the real world. It was his children's story about hobbits that led to a major epic fantasy and eventually gave him enough readers so that his earlier legends were publishable as *The Silmarillion*. But none of this was realized until years after he began writing the stories. Tolkien typed them up, not knowing where they would lead, and read them to his children. He progressed through Bilbo's adventure quite gradually. While he found ways to give his children closure, he did not have a real ending for it.

As the story progressed, Tolkien shared it with Lewis,

who loved it, especially the way it so perfectly described an imaginary world so that it seemed real. Tolkien appreciated the feedback and enjoyed his story, but he did not expect that it was really publishable. Even after reaching publishing success, Tolkien was always amazed at the popularity of his books.

Despite these low expectations, Tolkien also shared the story with others—including a student, Elaine Griffiths, who was at Oxford revising a translation of *Beowulf* for publication. Her friend from their college days, Susan Dagnall, came to visit her and discuss the manuscript. Susan worked as an editor for the London publisher Allen & Unwin, which was planning on publishing the translation of *Beowulf*. As Elaine and Susan talked, their conversation drifted to other topics, including a professor who had taught them both, Tolkien. Griffiths told Dagnall that she had read a wonderful children's story. Further, she even suggested that Dagnall should visit with him and see if she could get him to lend her the manuscript.

Tolkien was happy to let her borrow the manuscript, despite Dagnall's fears that he would not want to let it go. She read it on the train as she returned home and then sent it back a few days later. She wanted to show it to her superiors, she told Tolkien in a note, but the story would need to be finished before she could do so. This response, coming as it did just when Tolkien was on his long break and had a few weeks to spare, motivated him into a burst of productivity. By October 3, 1936, Tolkien had sent Dagnall a revised and completed manuscript. His son Michael helped him retype it, despite being temporarily only able to use one hand, due to an accident.[15]

## MONSTERS, CRITICS, AND EDITORS

Dagnall, as promised, passed the manuscript on to her superior, Stanley Unwin. He paid his son to review the manuscript and after hearing a good report agreed to publish it. It was not an easy process. In a day when revising typeset manuscripts had to be done by moving letter blocks by hand, Tolkien's habit of always finding new revisions to make could prove hugely expensive,[16] especially for a novel that, at the time, was considered a children's book.

Before much could be done in getting the manuscript ready for publication, however, Tolkien had to switch back from his side role as fantasy novelist to his profession as Oxford professor. On November 25, he gave a presentation at the Sir Israel Gollancz Memorial Lecture to the British Academy. He spoke on *Beowulf* and gave his speech the subtitle "The Monsters and the Critics."

Tolkien defended the integrity of the *Beowulf* story against critics who dismissed it as a mixture of various legends and stories. He pointed out how the story came to be written just at the moment when Christianity was spreading in the culture so that the legendary monsters became portrayed as the foes of God rather than as offspring of some of the gods. Tolkien compared Beowulf to the Cyclops Polyphemus, who was the offspring of Poseidon, to make his point. Christianity meant that evil creatures could not simply come from the true God, unlike the Cyclops, who came from the Greeks' god of the sea. Instead, they were God's enemies.[17]

Tolkien had a personal interest in what the author of

*Beowulf* had accomplished. As a Christian, he was using pre-Christian mythology and languages to build a series of stories about Middle-earth, and he was defending the author of *Beowulf* for doing the same thing.

Tolkien continued to work as a professor for the rest of 1936 and into 1937 while also trying to work with Allen & Unwin's editors to get the drafts into final form. Despite Tolkien's impulse to constantly change his material, they were able to get the manuscript ready for publication. However, they disagreed on the release date for the book. Tolkien had received a Leverhulme Research Fellowship in October of 1936, a grant he was to use for literary studies. He feared that his fellow professors would think he had used education funds in order to work on a moneymaking opportunity if the book came out near the end of that yearlong grant.[18] He thought a release in July would make it easier to convince his colleagues that he had not been misusing his time or the funds of the grant. But the publisher wanted to wait until September. Tolkien's revisions made the earlier date difficult. Also they wanted to release the book in a way that gave it the best chance of selling well. A fall release, when parents might be thinking about Christmas gifts, was much more sensible.

Behind Tolkien's desire for an earlier release date lurked a broader anxiety about his reputation as an academic. He was supposed to be a professor, not a novel writer. He was surrounded by people who prided themselves on teaching at one of the most prestigious schools in the world.[19]

The publisher's executives decided that Tolkien's concerns

were groundless. It was an easily verifiable matter that the book had been completed before his grant began, and there was no rule against spending one's own time on one's own project. Unwin's sense of timing and marketing paid off for Tolkien. They released the novel in September, and by Christmas 1937, the first run of *The Hobbit* had sold out.

# HOBBITS AND EPIC HEROISM (1938–1948)

T*he Hobbit* was an immediate success, but not yet the worldwide bestseller that would lead Tolkien to become the author of the century. Tolkien would need to write more to add to the story before that could happen. Stanley Unwin asked for a sequel. Could Tolkien write another story about hobbits?

Tolkien spent some time trying to get Allen & Unwin to publish *The Silmarillion*. But that wasn't what they wanted. The popularity of *The Hobbit* was not so great that Tolkien could guarantee the success of his next work. The publishers were looking for something that would interest a wide readership. To some extent, they still thought of *The Hobbit* as a kind of children's book, and the stories compiled in *The Silmarillion* were nothing of the kind. They were looking for a single coherent story to tell, whereas Tolkien's work was a compilation of stories. Even as a compilation, they were not complete. *The Silmarillion* manuscript needed much more work to finish than what had been done to finish *The Hobbit*.

Tolkien was not terribly surprised by this response. Though it was his life's work, he knew it wasn't likely to be appreciated by a wide audience. At least, there would not be a market for it until he had given the public real insight into what his fictional world might offer. So Tolkien set about right away working on a book to follow to *The Hobbit* before the end of 1937.

It took him twelve years to finish what would become *The Lord of the Rings*.

## MAKING FAIRY TALES GROW UP

In 1939, Tolkien was invited to be the speaker for the Andrew Lang Lecture in the University of St. Andrews in Scotland. Tolkien was able to speak with authority about his subject as a recent writer of a fantasy novel.

Reading the transcript of this lecture, entitled "On Fairy-Stories," one wonders how much of it reflects Tolkien's own issues in developing a sequel to *The Hobbit*. His book had featured a diminutive creature that seemed designed at first to appeal to children. Yet Tolkien spent much time in his lecture arguing that fairy stories should not only be for children. He began his lecture not as a fantasy author but as a philologist pointing out that the term "fairy-tale" or "fairy-story" was relatively new and thus hard to pin down. Tolkien questioned the recent definition of "fairy" as "of diminutive size." He argued that fairies were not "diminutive" but often quite grown-up at a time when he was struggling to write the sequel of what was widely regarded as a children's story. *The Hobbit* arguably wasn't really a children's story, but Tolkien didn't want there to be any confusion that it was a story for grown-ups.

After *The Lord of the Rings* was finally published, Tolkien remembered his lecture "On Fairy-Stories" as directly relevant to his work. While surprised at the popularity of the books, "it remains an unfailing delight to me to find my own belief justified: that the 'fairy-story' is really an adult genre, and one for which a starving audience exists," he wrote to a fan. "I said so, more or less, in my essay on the fairy-story. . . . But it was a mere proposition—which awaited proof." [1]

C. S. Lewis, wrote Tolkien, had said that the only way they were going to be able to read stories that they liked was to write them for themselves. [2] "Fairy-stories" in a way set out the test Tolkien wanted to pass—as Lewis did also. Lewis accomplished this feat quite early with his science fiction stories—and then later rapidly writing his Narnia Chronicles. But Tolkien simply could not operate that way. By the time he completed his final draft many years later, he claimed that he had typed through the entire manuscript at least twice. Parts were typed out more often, and much had been written over repeatedly by hand.

Tolkien had already begun to write more about the hobbits when he delivered his lecture on fairy stories, being very excited about producing another book and reaping the rewards. He wrote to Colin Furth, an editor at Allen & Unwin, "I have written the first chapter of a new story about

Hobbits—'A long expected party.'"[3] On February 4, 1938, he sent a copy of the chapter to be read by Stanley Unwin's son Rayner, the same boy who had originally reviewed *The Hobbit*. Rayner liked the chapter, and Tolkien was encouraged by this, but not enough to overcome his discouragement. He wasn't sure where this story should go. He wrote that, for him, it was "only too easy to write opening chapters—and for the moment the story is not unfolding."[4] A month later, however, he wrote that the sequel "has now progressed as far as the end of the third chapter. But stories tend to get out of hand, and this has taken an unpremeditated turn"—though he did not explain what turn this might be.[5]

Those directions did not turn out to be satisfying to Tolkien. Or he simply could not figure out where they were supposed to lead. On July 24, 1938, he sounded rather discouraged in his letter to Furth. He said that his work as a researcher had consumed both his time and his creativity. Work on the sequel had come to a halt. "It has lost my favour, and I have no idea what to do with it."[6]

Tolkien was pulled in two directions as a writer. On the one hand, his hobbits were entertaining to him and he could write about them and their lives in the Shire with a great deal of interest. One can still see this reading the first chapter of *The Fellowship of the Ring*. Tolkien could almost be classified as a humorist, both honoring and mocking English country life in the persons of his fictional creatures and their eating, drinking, gardening, and gossiping. Their naivete about the wider world and their self-satisfaction is both irritating and endearing. But he wrote to Furth that C. S. Lewis and others ("my most devoted fans") had assured him that the hobbits were only really interesting to others when they were described in "unhobbitlike" adventures.

On the other hand, he also felt the pull of the myths that would form *The Silmarillion*. This project continued to interest him, and he hinted once again about how he would like it to be published. He suggested that maybe he was incapable of writing a sequel until he had the "releasing effect" of getting the myths completed and published.

In retrospect the answer is obvious—just as this material leaked into *The Hobbit*, so his new hobbit story should present them as explorers in the wider world taking the reader with them. However, Tolkien hadn't thought through how to do that, and even though there was much to use in his *Silmarillion* stories, there wasn't enough to make it obvious how to proceed. He would need to add new layers to explain the third age of Middle-earth.

Despite expressing pessimism about having time to do much with the manuscript in late July, by the end of August he wrote that he was now on chapter 7.[7] Because he felt bad about not being able to give his publisher a complete sequel anytime soon, he submitted a short story, *Father Giles of Ham*, which did not get published until many years later. A little over a month later, he was able to report to Stanley Unwin that now ten chapters were done and he was working on the eleventh.[8] By now he knew that this book was to be much less of a child's book, for it was much more frightening than the first story. He said that he would be too busy to work on it for a while but still hoped he might complete it in the first few months of 1939.

Among the distractions Tolkien faced was the death of his friend E. V. Gordon, which was not only a personal loss but one that also entailed extra work teaching for Tolkien. Worse, war had broken in September, and Tolkien admitted that (though the work was not allegorical) the times may have put a shadow on the content of his writing. While those distractions were significant, the real problem is that Tolkien had not yet decided how to make a satisfactory sequel.

Thus far, this was a story about a hobbit named Bingo Baggins, who inherited Bilbo's Ring and who met a hobbit named Trotter in the inn at Bree.[9] Despite Tolkien's belief that this sequel was less childlike than *The Hobbit*, this version was much more like that first book than it was destined to become in final form. Sometime between October 1938 and February 1939, that changed. In his letter to editor Colin Furth, he reported on the story using the title it would have when the trilogy was published many years later, *The Lord of the Rings*.[10] He had finally come to the idea that the Ring was the one ruling Ring and that the diminutive hobbits were going to save the world—showing a real heroism even if it was not the same as that of mighty men.[11]

But this meant he had writing and rewriting to do before he got it right. Furthermore, it also meant following surprising turns in the story wherever they might lead. The book, far from remaining a single volume, became a gargantuan project that was not going to be publishable in the way that *The Hobbit* was published as one book.

## THE WAR AND AFTER

In the meantime, the years went by with Tolkien writing and rewriting, getting stuck, and then finding new ways of going forward. There was much to interrupt him. There were even intermittent times when he could not bear to deal with the story at all.

As the war progressed, his son Christopher joined the Royal Air Force and was stationed in South Africa. They stayed in touch, and Tolkien continued to share news of any progress he could make. In 1944, he wrote, "I wish I still had my amanuensis and critic near at hand"[12]—using the ancient Greek title for a letter-writer for someone else.

As the war ended, Tolkien went through another change: he was given the appointment of professor of English language and literature at Merton College. Like all Oxford dons, Tolkien worked for the university but held his position within one of the colleges that made up Oxford University. The position at Merton was a better fit for him at Oxford than his original position at Oxford's Pembroke College. Soon afterward the position of professor of English literature opened up, and many expected it to be offered to C. S. Lewis. When Lewis was passed over, a widening gap between Tolkien and Lewis began to become evident.[13]

While nothing dramatic happened between them (and there may be different views among contemporaries about how noticeable the break became and exactly when), the two men drifted apart—or perhaps drove each other apart. Lewis greatly aided Tolkien in working on *The Lord of the Rings* and getting it completed amid all the distractions and problems he ran into. When World War II started, Charles Williams moved to Oxford because the offices of his employer, Oxford University Press, were relocated there temporarily. Williams was the author of many books, some of which were novels that he and others dubbed "spiritual thrillers" in which artifacts possessed mystical powers. Lewis loved Williams's work and brought him to the Inklings, where he became a regular participant. Tolkien admitted to not understanding Williams's fiction at all. He was not happy that Williams began to come to meetings at the Eastgate Hotel on Monday nights, where Lewis and Tolkien had been meeting with each other weekly for more than ten years.[14]

Whether Tolkien's feelings about Williams were justified or not, Tolkien strove to act like a Christian gentleman. He found ways to appreciate Williams despite his distaste and frustration of Lewis paying so much attention to him. When Williams died suddenly in 1945, Tolkien assured his widow that he had "grown to admire and love your husband deeply" and was now "more grieved that I can express."[15]

But despite these honest words, what had come between Tolkien and Lewis was something that neither could overcome. Lewis was also different from Tolkien as a writer. He could rapidly write books, both fiction and nonfiction, while Tolkien was agonizing and rewriting from scratch.

In the realm of fantasy literature, even though Lewis was supportive, he was critical of some of the things that Tolkien loved and did not want to give up. On Tolkien's part, when

Lewis began writing his Narnia stories, Tolkien hated the mixing of different mythologies (such as Father Christmas and fauns of Greek mythology). He did not like the imaginary world of Narnia and told Lewis so. This could only further attenuate their relationship.

But in the meantime they remained cordial, and Lewis continued to encourage Tolkien in his literary efforts. Tolkien, for his part, kept working on the story despite distractions and stops. In 1947, he moved from Northmoor Road, where he and his family lived for so many years, and took up residence at a Merton College house on Manor Road. He did so because he now only had one remaining child—Priscilla—left with himself and Edith, and the Northmoor house was too big. But it wasn't long before he realized that he had made a mistake: the new house was too small. He would need to move when the opportunity presented itself.

By this time, despite less-than-ideal working conditions, he had come close to finishing *The Lord of the Rings*. This meant he had to produce a clean manuscript from all his pages and rewrites. He completed this in late 1949. And once this last task was finally completed, Tolkien had no one else to send it to for an appraisal other than C. S. Lewis, who had been so encouraging. It must have been very gratifying to read the letter from C. S. Lewis in response to the finished manuscript, concluding that "all the long years you have spent on it are justified."[16]

# THE WORLDWIDE
# BESTSELLER (1948–1973)

S o now Tolkien was done. His work was finished. And he had every reason to be confident that it would be published.

But this was not enough.

Tolkien finished his *Lord of the Rings* when he had found a way to write a story about the end of the third age that was consistent with his earlier writing project. Now that he had a work available that he knew was publishable and that he believed would appeal to audiences, he had a hard time letting go of his earlier work. Transforming his expected "new hobbit" story had increased his desire to get the previous history of Middle-earth available to readers. He wanted them both published together.

In order for Tolkien to get his *Lord of the Rings* published, he needed to let go of that desire. *The Silmarillion* only came out because so many readers fell in love with *The Lord of the Rings*. And despite the great demand for it, the work was not finished until Christopher Tolkien edited it for publication after his father died.

## THE PROBLEM OF DISTRUST (AND SOLVING IT)

In 1949, Tolkien was having a hard time being realistic about what he could accomplish. Allen & Unwin had hoped for a long time for a sequel to *The Hobbit*, but Tolkien was losing faith in their willingness to do justice to his work—which he partly measured by a willingness to publish *The Silmarillion*. Part of the trouble came from the shorter story, *Farmer Giles of Ham*. Allen & Unwin had finally published that story as a book in 1949. But Tolkien found the quality of the book lacking and thought the company should have done a better job promoting the book. He was also frustrated when the publisher released a new run of *The Hobbit* that lacked the color pictures in the original.

Perhaps Tolkien would not have been swayed to leave his publisher if he hadn't been presented with an alternative. But temptation came to him through the Inklings. One occasional member of the group was a Roman Catholic priest named Gervase Matthew. He introduced Tolkien to fellow Roman Catholic Milton Waldman, who worked for Collins publishers. While Matthew was interested in Tolkien as a known author and member of a known literary circle, William Collins, the owner of the publishing company, was particularly hoping to persuade Tolkien to switch to his firm to produce future editions of *The Hobbit*. But he naturally did not introduce himself to Tolkien with this proposal. He simply said he was interested in a sequel.

In late 1949, Tolkien sent him a partially typed and partially handwritten manuscript, not of *The Lord of the Rings*, but of *The Silmarillion*. Would he be interested in publishing this work? Waldman said he would be interested in publishing the finished work once Tolkien completed it. Having met these standards, Tolkien was then willing to send him the manuscript for *The Lord of the Rings*. As much as this work was different from *The Hobbit*, it was much more accessible than *The Silmarillion*.

As an ambassador for his publisher, one who was supposed to attract authors, Waldman could tell Tolkien truthfully that Collins was not just a publisher, but also a seller of stationery and journals. They had, therefore, more paper on hand than other publishing companies. By design or accident, Tolkien understood this to mean that the supply of paper would not be a concern. This was a misunderstanding of how company expenses work. As it turned out, despite expressing interest, when confronted with the monstrous amount of material that would be involved in releasing both *The Silmarillion* and *The Lord of the Rings*, the publisher did want Tolkien to make cuts in his manuscript.

This whole process was again slowed down by Tolkien's other duties and by events that distracted him. In 1950, he moved again, this time to a house on Holywell Street that gave him more usable space. He kept working partially as his new publisher wanted: Tolkien tried to make cuts in *The Lord of the Rings* but in the meantime kept sending more material to go into *The Silmarillion*. Eventually, in 1952, still without a signed contract, Tolkien demanded that Collins hurry up and publish *The Lord of the Rings* or else he would go elsewhere. The publisher let him go. Tolkien was now back where he had started.

Tolkien swallowed his pride and wrote a letter of query to Allen & Unwin asking if they were still interested in the work. He dropped his requirement that *The Silmarillion* be published with it.

Rayner Unwin, the original reviewer of *The Hobbit*, was now grown up and working with his father's company. He welcomed Tolkien back and found a way to publish *The Lord of the Rings* in full, without making any of the cuts that Tolkien had been told to make for Collins. He, too, felt the problem of expensive paper, which meant that larger books were less profitable. Furthermore, Tolkien's last book was now more than a decade in the past. While he recognized the merit of *The Lord of the Rings*, he also knew it was a much different book from *The Hobbit* and he had no way of knowing how the public would respond. He could not afford to be stuck with big, unsold books that would cost him so much.

Unwin believed that the best course was to publish the work as three books and to do so in a nontraditional arrangement. Rather than use the typical royalty contract, he suggested that Tolkien share in half of all the profits but not make any money on the sales of the books until the publisher had recouped all costs of publishing the run. This promised a much greater profit to Tolkien if the books sold well. On the other hand, if they did not sell well, Tolkien would not get any royalties— but this would also minimize Allen & Unwin's losses. Tolkien agreed with this and, in so doing, provided the world with an uncut edition of his work.

From a business standpoint for Allen & Unwin, though the risk was diminished, it was still substantial. Rayner had to ask permission from his father and admitted to him they could lose a thousand pounds. His father agreed to publish it, in part no doubt because Rayner was a true believer in Tolkien's work.[1] He wanted to publish it and told his father it was a work of genius.

## BECOMING FAMOUS: OF PIRACY
## AND PUBLICITY

By the time the first volume, *The Fellowship of the Ring*, came out in the summer of 1954, the Tolkiens had been living for about a year in a new home on Sandfield Road, two miles outside of Oxford. Only six weeks after the initial publication, a reprint was ordered. The second volume came out in November and again sold well. Houghton Mifflin published both works in the United States.

But the final volume was not complete because Tolkien had promised some explanatory appendices that were not yet written. Here again his perfectionism and interest in his fictional world, the very forces that produced such a great work, were conspiring against him to prevent its publication. He overcame them, however, but not without stringing out readers for longer than they expected. He received anxious letters both from readers and his publisher. *The Return of the King* was not published until almost a year after the first volume came out.

Though most know *The Lord of the Rings* only as a worldwide phenomenon, that success came in stages and suffered from some exceptions. The main exceptions were found in the reviews of some critics. While C. S. Lewis raved about the book and W. H. Auden loved it, other reviewers, such as Edwin Muir and Edmund Wilson, were quite hostile toward the books. One of the issues, ironically, was the advocacy of C. S. Lewis. Now well-known as a Christian apologist, Lewis was a controversial figure. While many loved him, there were others who felt quite the opposite about his writing. Having Lewis as a champion virtually guaranteed the provocation of strong feelings among the literati, much of it negative.

Despite Lewis's strong promotion of the book, the personal gap between Tolkien and Lewis continued to widen, especially when Lewis married Joy Davidman in 1957. As a Roman Catholic, it troubled Tolkien that Lewis had married a divorcée. He was also unhappy that his bachelor friend now had a wife, which added further complications to their relationship. Lewis had often kept Tolkien out many nights as if he had no home life to go back to. Now that Lewis had a home life to distract him, he could no longer be as devoted to their friendship. However, as a sincere Christian, Tolkien did not allow his cooling relationship with Lewis to start any public feud or damage Lewis's reputation.

But the good reviews overcame the bad reviews among the public, and the books sold much better than *The Hobbit* ever had and even promoted the earlier novel to many who had missed it. Back in 1938, after *The Hobbit* had first been released, it sold about three thousand copies in the United States and three thousand in Great Britain. This was a success, but it didn't make a dramatic difference in Tolkien's financial life. His *Lord of the Rings* was receiving many more reviews and making a great many more sales.

Tolkien began to see a financial return in 1956 and found it to be a challenge due to the British "progressive" taxation rate. He received a check for more than his yearly salary as an Oxford professor, and each check thereafter was larger until 1965.[2] Due to the pressures of higher taxes, Tolkien was quick to sell his original manuscripts of *The Hobbit*, *The Lord of the Rings*, *Farmer Giles of Ham*, and the unpublished children's story "Mr. Bliss" to Marquette University, a Jesuit school in Milwaukee, Wisconsin.[3] The acquisition of these manuscripts was because of an aggressive director of libraries for the institution, William B. Ready, who had faith that Tolkien's work would have long-lasting and worldwide value to literature.[4] He bought the documents for less than the equivalent of 5,000 dollars in American currency (at 1957 values).[5]

Tolkien retired in 1959. He had let his friendship with Lewis fade. From some time in the middle of the 1950s, he ceased being part of male circles of intellectuals and became a homebody. This new life was partly helped by the distance of his house from the campus and also by the decline in Edith's health.[6] When Lewis died in 1963, Tolkien expressed sadness to his daughter Priscilla "that we should have been so separated in the last years," but expressed confidence that "our time of close communion endured in memory for both of us."[7] It was sadly ironic that Lewis died before seeing the full flowering of Tolkien's fame since he had encouraged him so much to persevere in his work.

While sales were good for Tolkien for several years, providing him with better retirement income than he had ever expected, in 1965 a new wave of popularity swept across the United States that launched him into a new level of success. An unauthorized version of *The Lord of the Rings* caused a drastic increase in readership among youth. The problem was that Tolkien was not offered any royalties from the book.

The book sales might have increased earlier if Tolkien's official publisher had paid more attention to the market and invested in new opportunities. Tolkien was already doing better than he had ever expected, and even though he cared enough about his readers to spend hours answering their letters, he was still overcome with amazement that so many people were reading his books at all. His publisher was content to sell the hardback edition of *The Lord of the Rings*. Such was the situation almost a decade after the publication of *The Lord of the Rings*: the only way for Americans to purchase it was to pay for the three volumes in hardback. Meanwhile, the editors of Ace Books noticed that the story was growing in popularity among students. But if more students were purchasing the book despite the expense, what would happen if a much cheaper edition became available? They saw a tremendous potential and wanted to take advantage of it.

By the copyright law that was in place at that time, Houghton Mifflin imported unbound sheets from Allen & Unwin in Britain and stitched them together under their own book cover. But they were only permitted to import a limited number, which Ace found they had exceeded. The decision makers at Ace decided to produce their own paperback version for seventy-five cents a volume. They declared that the story was now public domain since Houghton Mifflin had violated the law.

When Stanley Unwin realized what Ace was going to do, he took immediate action. He could not take legal action that would stop Ace. Nor could he simply publish *The Lord of the Rings* as it was, because that would simply be an attempt to sell a public domain work. Since they would need to pay Tolkien royalties, they probably could not sell as cheap a volume. What they needed was an authentic edition of *The Lord of the Rings* to which they had a defendable copyright. The only way to do this was to get Tolkien to make some revisions in the manuscript so that it was a different entity.

Tolkien was now seventy-three years old and was not as accustomed to sudden concentrated effort. Stanley Unwin left Tolkien's home thinking that he understood how dire it was that they get a new revised manuscript. But instead of revising *The Lord of the Rings*, he kept working on side projects. Then, months later, he turned not to *The Lord of the Rings* but to *The Hobbit*. This was not as important because Ace was not producing a version of that book and Tolkien still had control of that copyright. The irony is that Ballantine, which was working with Houghton Mifflin, decided they could not wait and produced the original version of *The Hobbit*. It was not until late 1965 that a new American paperback version of *The Lord of the Rings* was published. By then the Ace edition had already been published and was selling well.

It turned out that the Ace "piracy" was the best thing that could have happened to turn Tolkien from a bestselling author to an international phenomenon. In the first place, their low-priced edition reached about a hundred thousand customers. That was a sudden stimulus to word-of-mouth advertising so that, when the Ballantine edition came out for ninety-five cents a volume, they sold ten times that number in a short time thereafter. The controversy itself generated additional publicity in the media so that people who had never heard of Tolkien got curious and found that it was worth the low price to see what was so attractive about Tolkien that a publisher had "pirated" him.

Furthermore, the Ace book did not substantially compete with Tolkien's edition with Ballantine. Tolkien was a meticulous correspondent with virtually everyone who sent him mail. In many cases, these letter-writers with questions would know other Tolkien fans or be part of clubs. Once Tolkien began to make a point of complaining about how Ace was publishing *The Lord of the Rings* without his permission or giving him any compensation, the word spread among fans. Ace's sales fell because many felt it was worth the twenty cents extra to support Tolkien. In addition, Ace felt pressure from groups like the

Tolkien Society of America and the Science Fiction Writers of America.[8] They soon announced that they would cease selling the book once the printing ran out. They also offered to pay a royalty to Tolkien for every copy they sold.

Without Ace Books, no one knows when the publishers might have decided it was time to produce a cheap paperback edition of Tolkien's works. As it was, Ace did a valuable entrepreneurial service for Tolkien, risking money on the gamble that the bestselling book could appeal to an even wider audience— that the market was not already saturated. Not paying anything to Tolkien was morally questionable, but Tolkien's own readers helped him out at a time when the law had nothing to say in the matter. As it stands, Tolkien made far more money from Ace's work—even if they hadn't paid him any royalties for the books they sold—than he would have otherwise. It is worth noting that Ace showed more care about the work than Ballantine did. While Ace had produced well-designed books with relevant cover art, Ballantine engaged an artist who knew nothing of the story. He produced a picture of a fruit tree and emus for the cover of *The Fellowship of the Ring*.[9] Tolkien told at least one witness that he was "glad for the Ace Books controversy because it kept Mr. Ballantine on his toes."[10]

## THE GRAY HAVENS

When Lewis died, Tolkien reported that, up until that point, he had been feeling normal for his age, "like an old tree that is losing all its leaves one by one." But the death of Lewis was more like the chop of an ax biting into the tree's roots.[11] Yet Tolkien experienced his greatest fame at a time when his gifts and abilities were in decline.

It was not that he was unable to complete any projects. In 1964, he got *Tree and Leaf* published—though both the works it contained were from years earlier. In addition to a written form of his lecture "On Fairy-Stories," Tolkien's "Leaf by Niggle" was included in that work. It had been first published in 1945 in the *Dublin Review* and was probably the closest thing to an allegory that Tolkien ever wrote. It was about an artist named Niggle who, in his attempt to portray a leaf, ended up forced to draw a whole tree and then a whole landscape around it so that he could never finish the project. The story was about Tolkien's own inability to create a sequel to *The Hobbit* when he was frustrated and afraid he would never finish it.

But Tolkien was facing the same problem all over again. Now that he was virtually a cult figure, there was great interest in the history behind *The Hobbit* and *The Lord of the Rings*. His dream could come true. Any book publishing company would love to publish *The Silmarillion*. But he never could finish it. It was now a collection of stories in various states—being written or being rewritten. Clyde Kilby, who worked as an assistant for him, says that he found Tolkien to be "a Barliman Butterbur, looking here and there for portions of *The Silmarillion*" among boxes of papers crowding his office.[12] Part of the problem was that *The Lord of the Rings* had gone beyond *The Silmarillion*, requiring histories of Ents and Galadriel and other new facets of Middle-earth. And he knew that if he missed a detail, readers would pounce on it.[13] While *The Silmarillion* had made *The Lord of the Rings* possible, *The Lord of the Rings* had forced a transformation onto *The Silmarillion*.

Kilby's appraisal in 1967 was that there was no way Tolkien would ever complete *The Silmarillion*. He did get a chance to read Tolkien's short story *Smith of Wootton Major* and confirmed that it should be published. That story came about because Tolkien was supposed to write an introduction to George Macdonald's *The Golden Key*. But rereading the story, Tolkien found he no longer appreciated Macdonald and, instead of writing an introduction, produced his own Fairyland story.

In that case, Tolkien's impulses resulted in a publishable story. But in many cases, he involved himself in minutiae that had little to do with his real writing projects. Clyde Kilby tried in vain in the summer of 1967 to get Tolkien to write a preface to his translations of *The Pearl* and *Sir Gawain and the Green Knight*. Yet it was never finished, and the translations were not published until after Tolkien's death. The perfectionism that had burdened him earlier in life had now reached a point of no return. It would be his son Christopher's job to release material and write prefaces.

But Tolkien's time was well spent in these days taking care of his wife. He was now in a position to afford many comforts. In 1968, he made the unprecedented move from Oxford to Poole near Bournemouth, a seaside resort in the south of England. There was virtually nothing about Bournemouth that appealed to him as a place to live, but he and Edith had vacationed there at the Miramar hotel. He noticed that she enjoyed herself there and felt much less isolated than she did at Oxford. Since Tolkien was taking her to the hotel to give her a rest from housekeeping, it occurred to him that if they moved nearby they could visit more often. So, for once, the Tolkiens moved for the sake of Edith primarily, rather than for the sake of Tolkien's career.

Despite Tolkien's dilemma to relax or to try to produce material, his and Edith's time there was restful. She died three years after they moved, on November 29, 1971, after being hospitalized with an inflamed gall bladder. She was eighty-two years old.

Despite Edith's age, the quickness of her death was a surprise for Tolkien. Since he had no reason to remain in Bournemouth, he moved back to Oxford. Merton College made him a residential honorary fellow, which meant his life was now circling back to when he was a member of the T.C.B.S. He was once again living in campus rooms. He had his own scout to serve his needs, and he could eat at high table or visit in the common room. Tolkien visited his children and grandchildren and also his brother. On his way to visit friends at Bournemouth, he became sick from an acute bleeding gastric ulcer. This led to an infection, and he died on September 2, 1973.

# LEGACY

peaking of his writing journey, John Flanagan, author of the series Ranger's Apprentice, has said that he and other fantasy authors owe a debt to J. K. Rowling and her Harry Potter books.[1] Readers can see how much the debt is also owed to J. R. R. Tolkien. The name of Flanagan's series and the vocation of his protagonist are a salute to Tolkien's influence, which made the word *ranger* a commonplace term for a lone hero of an epic quasi-medieval world.

Even apart from Rowling's confessed familiarity with Tolkien, her fiction by itself shows his influence.[2] It is hard to imagine Dumbledore without there first being a Gandalf. And Rowling, like Tolkien, presented an alternative reality with its own rules and its own portrayal of love and loyalty fighting against political idiocy (the Ministry of Magic) and real evil (Voldemort). In an age when scholars complain that we are fragmenting because not enough of us watch the same mainstream newscaster, J. K. Rowling's fiction showed that massive numbers of people all over the world could respond to a vision of epic heroism in what began as children's literature. Tolkien himself had already done the same thing: he produced a mythology that was internalized all over the world. In both cases, people acquired a shared cultural background in an imaginary culture.

One can also understand Tolkien's immense influence by comparing what happened to Gary Gygax, the cocreator of the Dungeons and Dragons role-playing game. Gygax was part of a subculture of gaming that devoted time and money to playing relatively esoteric miniature war games. When asked in an interview if he expected his role-playing game to be so successful, he replied:

> When I wrote the D&D game in 1972-3 I envisaged an audience of military board gamers, military miniatures players, and fantasy, SF and horror fans only. This was indeed the initial core audience, and it wasn't until 1976, two years after the game was first sold, that I began to realize that the appeal was more universal.[3]

Tolkien's contribution to the genre of fantasy is similar— he didn't just write for those who already read the genre. The universal appeal of Tolkien's fantasy may well be an important reason why there is now a plethora of fantasy books in the science fiction section of any bookstore. Terry Brooks, a popular author of many fantasy stories, was asked about Tolkien's influence on him. "I don't know if we can measure Tolkien's impact. Every writer of modern fantasy was influenced by Tolkien to some degree," he said. "He was the premiere fantasy writer of the last century, and all of us writing today owe him a huge debt."[4] Tolkien both inspired new creative writers and demonstrated that there was a market for their work.

Even the popularity of Gygax's game may have been due in large part to the popularity of Tolkien. While Gygax himself was reading *Conan* and other sword and sorcery stories long before Tolkien and came up with his game system apart from Tolkien, he realized he would be hurting himself if he did not involve the major monsters and races of Middle-earth in the game. "Just about all the players were huge JRRT fans, and so they insisted that I put as much Tolkien-influenced material into the game as possible." The first D&D game had Balrogs, Ents, and hobbits, which later had to be changed for copyright reasons but were still obvious Tolkien creations: Balor demons, Treants, and Halflings.[5]

## TOLKIEN, THE WORLD-FAMOUS CHRISTIAN AUTHOR

In 1997, the British bookstore chain Waterstone's polled readers for their opinion of the best book of the twentieth century. *The Lord of the Rings* was voted the best book, ahead of George Orwell's *1984* and *Animal Farm*, ahead of James Joyce's *Ulysses*, and ahead of Harper Lee's *To Kill a Mockingbird*.[6] Not only did *The Lord of the Rings* win first place in the overall survey, but it came in first in 104 out of 105 bookstores where the survey was taken.[7] In the twenty-first century Tolkien continues to enjoy iconic status.

Between *The Lord of the Rings* and *The Hobbit*, Peter Jackson's 6 movies represent the most awarded film series in history, winning 475 gongs out of 800 nominations across all ceremonies. . . . Each *The Lord of the Rings* release improved upon the box office of its predecessor, and the three films became the highest grossing movie trilogy of all time by beating the original *Star Wars* trilogy, and remaining so in 2020.[8]

It is worth pondering, especially for Christians with an interest in literature, why Tolkien's work remains so popular. While both Lewis and Williams wrote books that were identifiably Christian, both in fiction and in nonfiction, Tolkien's approach was different. He wrote novels that were set in a pre-Christian past and were surprisingly secular in the sense that there were no prayers or religious rituals or events. As is commonly pointed out, they contain no reference to Christianity.

Or they contained *almost* no reference. In *The Return of the King*, when Gandalf is confronting a despairing ruler trying to commit suicide and kill his wounded son so that they are joined together in death, the wizard rebukes him, denying he has the authority to decide how and when he will die. Then Gandalf reminds him that this was how past heathen rulers would act who were enslaved to Sauron, "the Dark Power." They would then kill themselves in despair and take others with them to comfort themselves in their dying. Tolkien's love for ancient Christian hero stories like *Beowulf* shows up here in his own writing, where his language implies there has been a conversion from paganism to Christianity.

## NOT AN AGENDA BUT A VISION

As a Christian, Tolkien believed that all truth was from God and that it even pushed itself into human culture through myths and legends. This was a point Tolkien made with C. S. Lewis that fateful night when Lewis was struggling with Christianity. Just because myths did not happen does not mean they don't relate truth. Thus, in writing a myth for the modern world, Tolkien was rather confident that he was somehow reflecting God's truth, even without explicitly mentioning him. As God was the Creator, humans made in his image were meant to be sub-creators. But these works of sub-creation were not truly independent because God is the original author of all things. They derive truth from the source of all truth.

While myths could be used wrongly, Tolkien could avoid such misuse as a Christian and write a myth that was not mere allegory but still communicated truth.

Tolkien claimed his Ring fiction had no inner meaning or message. He denied it was allegorical or topical—for Tolkien, the point was to let readers make their own choices. Tolkien's claim that he had disliked allegory in all its manifestations makes sense when one considers his point of distinguishing allegory from applicability. Applicability is different because it resides in the freedom in the reader, he said, not in the purposed domination of the author. Having written an epic of good versus evil,

Tolkien left readers free to make up their own minds how to apply his fiction.

Tolkien presented the reader with a vision of a fallen world, in which there was evil to overcome and also the realization that the ultimate evil, or death, could not be overcome by heroism. But it was a world in which there was much beauty and where there was true courage to do what was right even at great cost. Tolkien portrayed a fantasy world that could not only entertain us but could also challenge and inspire us.

## TOLKIEN'S WORLD: ANTIMODERN AND ANTITOTALITARIAN

Aspects of Tolkien's vision tempt some to write him off as a Luddite, someone opposed to technological development as an evil thing. Virtually every piece of machinery in *The Lord of the Rings* is associated with the innovations of Sauron or those of Saruman in a quest for power over others. Tolkien loved trees and hated seeing the countryside reduced to make room for new developments. Though he owned a motorcycle for a time and then later an automobile, he came to detest these things because their increasing usage demanded more paving over the country-side that he loved. It is no accident that Tolkien became wildly popular among students who tended to have environmentalist concerns and values.

But while Tolkien despised certain developments, he would not have stopped them or thought that someone ought to try to stop them all. He tended to be humble about what sort of influence he believed he could have on the world. That is why most of the evidence of what he believed on many topics is only available through private letters that have been collected. Not only was Tolkien opposed to "dominating the reader" through allegory; he hated dominating others through politics as well.

Tolkien described his politics to his son Christopher as tending "more and more to anarchy"—which he was quick to point out did not mean, for him, any kind of terrorism but was to be understood as "abolition of control."[9] Yet he was, alternatively, an "unconstitutional monarchist."[10] The rise of large bureaucratic states was a feature of the modern world, and not just in the fascism that the Allies fought against during World War II. Tolkien wanted an end to the practice of referring to the government "with a capital *G*," and he also wanted to abolish the use of the word "State." Instead, he wanted people to clearly understand who their rulers were, if they were indeed rulers. Better to refer to a king by name as one's ruler and recognize the authority of the relationship, than to refer to an abstraction like the Government or the State in which the actual personal authority gets hidden in a faceless impersonal bureaucracy.

Tolkien's convictions came from a suspicion of organizations claiming to act as agents of "the people." Such a claim provides a pretense that there is no authoritarianism. "The People" are engaged in "self-rule" through their agents. But some people are still ordering the lives of other people and determining their fates. Naming these rulers, rather than resorting to fake entities like "the State," would "go a long way to clearing thought."[11]

Even though Tolkien's story involved *The Return of the King*, Tolkien had doubts about such personal rulers as well. Tolkien told his son that not "even saints" were good at "bossing" others. "Not one in a million is fit for it, and least of all those who seek the opportunity."[12]

This fluctuation between kings and "anarchy" is not odd for a student of northern European tribal history. As a scholar who had lectured on *Beowulf* and had read Old Icelandic literature, Tolkien knew all about the kings and chieftains as he wrote about in Middle-earth. And Tolkien was also aware of medieval Iceland, a society that had lasted for centuries, both as a pagan society and then as a Christian one, without any centralized state at all. Iceland had a self-perpetuating system of private law that involved no taxation, no military, and no prisons. One legal scholar described Iceland this way:

Iceland is known to most men as a land of volcanoes, geysers and glaciers. But it ought to be no less interesting to the student of history as the birthplace of a brilliant literature in poetry and prose, and as the home of a people who have maintained for many centuries a high level of intellectual cultivation. It is an almost unique instance of a community whose culture and creative power flourished independently of any favouring material conditions, and indeed under conditions in the highest degree unfavourable. Nor ought it to be less interesting to the student of politics and laws as having produced a Constitution unlike any other whereof records remain, and a body of law so elaborate and complex that it is hard to believe that it existed among men whose chief occupation was to kill one another.[13]

So Tolkien's statement that he veered between anarchism and real dynastic monarchy (as opposed to a constitutional monarchy) makes a great deal of sense. It also makes sense of the constant temptation involved in the one Ring—the temptation of power. Even Galadriel refuses this, though Frodo offers her the power: "I will diminish, and go into the West, and remain Galadriel."[14] She does this even though she could do much good with the Ring of Power. "I wish you'd take his Ring," Sam Gamgee says. "You'd put things to rights. You'd stop them digging up the gaffer and turning him adrift." Sam is referring to a vision of the Shire he was given, in which not only was his father turned out of his home, but many trees were destroyed. Galadriel could stop this from happening with the Ring. He says, "You'd make some folks pay for their dirty work." "I would," Galadriel agrees with Sam. "That is how it would begin. But it would not stop with that, alas!"[15]

In seeing how Tolkien portrays the danger of power, it is helpful to again think about his experience with war and its aftermath. As one who lived through a bloody conflict that took away many of his friends and changed the political structure of Europe from kingdoms and empires to parliamentary democracies, Tolkien didn't feel that this change was all for the better. Rather than rant about it or get publicly frustrated, he wrote a novel in which authority was personal and power over others was a temptation rather than a virtue. Tolkien wrote in one letter that he started an attempt on a sequel that took place a century after the fall of Mordor. He did not continue with it, he said, because it "proved both sinister and depressing." Human nature, he said, meant that "the people of Gondor in times of peace, justice, and prosperity, would become discontented and restless—while the dynasts descended from Aragorn would become just kings and governors—like Denethor or worse."[16]

So if Tolkien had a pessimistic appraisal of human nature and the possibility of preserving a free society, his fiction still presents readers with a vision of freedom, the faithfulness necessary to fight for it, and the temptations that must be resisted.

## NOT ESCAPISM BUT EQUIPPING

Tolkien was not alone, even though he was uniquely successful, in his fantasy story. In his excellent work *J. R. R. Tolkien: Author of the Century*, Tom Shippey, a successor to Tolkien academically, points out:

The dominant literary mode of the twentieth century has become the fantastic. This may appear a surprising claim, which would not have seemed even remotely conceivable at the start of the century and which is bound to encounter fierce resistance even now. However, when the time comes to look back at the century, it seems very likely that future literary historians, detached from the squabbles of our present, will see as its most representative and distinctive works books like J.R.R. Tolkien's *The Lord of the Rings*.[17]

He goes on to list many other authors of the fantastic: George Orwell, William Golding, Kurt Vonnegut, Ursula Le Guin, and Thomas Pynchon. Shippey was writing early enough that he probably did not realize how huge a phenomenon the Harry Potter books would be.[18]

Claiming that the popularity of fantasy is evidence of escapism is a common rationale among many academic critics. A key assumption in this argument is that modern readers are using Tolkien's world of epic fantasy to escape from the world. It is likely that rather than *escaping* from the modern world to an imaginary realm of heroic epic, readers feel that the stories portray a *reality* that gives them tools or encouragement for living in the modern world. Instead of being simplistic, Tolkien's epics provide exactly the mythic resource that people need to live in a complex world. Dealing with the temptation of power, fighting for what's right, persevering in faithfulness, and many other issues that are portrayed in *The Lord of the Rings* are not irrelevant to the modern world.

If fantasy literature in general has been used to benefit readers in this way, and this is a reason why the genre has been so important in the last century, then the popularity of Tolkien's works may be a subtle argument for the power of Christ. Even though not explicitly Christian, Tolkien's books about diminutive, middle-class, unheroic creatures have outsold many works featuring muscle-bound warriors, clever thieves, and powerful magicians. If readers are turning to fantasy to deal with reality, what can it mean that they continue to turn to this particular epic fantasy more consistently over the decades than to any other?

## TOLKIEN'S EPITAPH AND HIS LIFE IN MIDDLE-EARTH

The last word from his fantasy creation that was written at Tolkien's direction was the one word, "Beren." It is etched on his tombstone, which he shared with the remains of his wife, Edith. Under her name is the name of "Luthien."[19] He had written very early a story of Beren and Luthien. When Edith died and he chose to put the name on his tombstone, he wrote an explanation to his son Christopher, denying that this was a mere "pet name" as one might read about in obituaries.

> I never called Edith Luthien—but she was the source of the story that in time became the chief plan of the *Silmarillion*. It was first conceived in a small woodland glade filled with hemlocks at Roos in Yorkshire (where I was for a brief time in command of an outpost of the Humber Garrison in 1917, and she was able to live with me for awhile). In those days her hair was raven, her skin clear, her eyes brighter than

you have seen them, and she could sing—and *dance*. But the story has gone crooked.[20]

The story went crooked ultimately because of death and all the sin and decay leading to it. But it was still a majestic story, and Tolkien found the material for it in his own domestic life. While one can rightly read *The Lord of the Rings* and all of Tolkien's epic fiction as a saga about war and good and evil, it applied just as well to the courageous heroism required of every man and woman to simply live in the world with all its splendor and ugliness and the struggle between.

Tolkien's use of his own private experiences in creating his epic fantasy give us more evidence that the key to his success lies in his humility in refusing to moralize to his readers. He did not wish to dominate his readers because he wanted them to be free to see their own lives in the adventures that he described. Even though world war and Tolkien's experiences in the face of real battles are part of what created his story, one does not need to experience life during wartime to relate to, learn from, and use Tolkien's fiction. The loves and losses that we all experience in peacetime as well as in wartime are more than sufficient to make his imagined world relevant to ours. His enduring impact on the world shows us how a Christian artist can be most effective when he offers himself rather than when he tries to "help" others see the truth. While God calls Christians to proclaim his truth in a variety of ways and situations—some of which are unavoidably confrontational—we can learn from Tolkien that sometimes a mere story can change people's lives.

# JOURNEY TO MIDDLE-EARTH

## Book Club Discussion Questions

1. Did this book inspire you to read J. R. R. Tolkien if you haven't before? Which book do you want to read first? If you have read Tolkien's works before, does it make you want to revisit them? If so, why?

2. How have Tolkien's works had an impact on society culturally, specifically regarding the prevalence of the fantasy genre in fiction, movies, and television? Is society better or worse off with Tolkien's works in it?

3. Tolkien was a master at world-building. His Middle-earth is like no other setting in fiction. How is Middle-earth reminiscent of the world Tolkien grew up in? How is it different from our own world?

4. Tolkien's experience with loss and tragedy carries over into his fiction, and his books reflect the ramifications of such emotional upheaval. What are some instances where loss, tragedy, and disappointment have a profound effect on specific characters?

5. Tolkien's father Arthur died when Ronald was only four years old, and his mother passed away eight years later. How do you think becoming orphaned by the age of twelve affected Tolkien's writing? How do you think it affected his faith?

6. Tolkien clearly had a vivid imagination, capable of

creating a vast, diverse world filled with fascinating creatures and a remarkably distinctive society populated by heroes, villains, and regular folks. What does the depth of his imagination reveal about creativity itself? How are creativity and faith inextricably linked?

7. How is friendship revealed as a significant theme, both in Tolkien's own life and in the plots of his novels?

8. Tolkien's narrative style is rich with detail. As a reader, do you prefer sprawling descriptions and vivid world-building, or would you rather the scenes be simpler and more concise? Why or why not?

9. If you had to select one Tolkien title as your favorite, which book would it be and why?

10. Tolkien was quite familiar with loss, from both his childhood and during his World War I experience. How do you think his familiarity with death played out in his writing?

11. Which movie or screen adaptation based on Tolkien's writings is your favorite? Why?

12. During the "Great War," Tolkien encountered the violence and carnage of combat. How do you think this firsthand experience informed the narrative of *The Lord of the Rings* trilogy?

13. Who is your favorite Tolkien character and why?

14. Some readers believe *The Hobbit* is Tolkien's most successful novel, while others think the *LOTR* trilogy holds that distinction. Which one do you support, or is there another Tolkien work you would argue for? Why?

15. Who are the three most important characters in Tolkien's canon and why?

16. Tolkien was a gifted linguist and a professional philologist, that is, an expert in the study of languages. How do you think this expertise and background contributed to his creation of the Middle-earth universe?

17. Which Tolkien character are you most like and why?

18. What are some main themes found throughout Tolkien's books that have resonated with you?

19. Tolkien's influences include William Shakespeare, Charles Dickens, H. G. Wells, and Jules Verne, just to name a few. Where do you see their influence in his writings?

20. How have J. R. R. Tolkien's writings inspired you? How have they inspired the world?

# NOTES

## INTRODUCTION

1. Humphrey Carpenter, *Tolkien: A Biography* (New York: Houghton Mifflin, 2000), 215.
2. Tom Fish, "The 30 Best Selling Books of All Time," *Newsweek*, September 13, 2021, https://www.newsweek.com/best-selling -books-all-time-1628133.
3. Tracy Mumford, "Literary Mysteries: The Best-selling Books of All Time," MPR (Minnesota Public Radio) News, July 21, 2015, https://www.mprnews.org/story/2015/07/21/thread-books-bcst -best-selling-books.
4. Anthony Breznican and Joanna Robinson, "Amazon's *Lord of the Rings* Series Rises: Inside *The Rings of Power*," *Vanity Fair*, February 10, 2022, https://www.vanityfair.com/hollywood/2022 /02/amazon-the-rings-of-power-series-first-look.

## CHAPTER 1

1. Carpenter, *Tolkien: A Biography*, 21.
2. Letter to W. H. Auden, June 7, 1955, in Humphrey Carpenter, ed., *The Letters of J. R. R. Tolkien* (London: Allen & Unwin, 1981), 217.
3. J. R. R. Tolkien, *The Annotated Hobbit* (New York: Houghton Mifflin, 1988), 169.
4. Carpenter, *Tolkien: A Biography*, 22.
5. Ibid., 23.
6. Ibid.
7. Joseph Pearce, *Tolkien: Man and Myth* (Fort Collins, CO: Ignatius Press, 2001), 14.
8. Colin Duriez, *Tolkien and C. S. Lewis: The Gift of Friendship* (Mahwah, NJ: Paulist Press, 2003), 5.
9. André Haynal, "Childhood Lost and Recovered," *International Forum of Psychoanalysis* 12, no. 1 (2003): 30–37.
10. Mark Kanzer, "Writers and the Early Loss of Parents," *Journal*

*of the Hillside Hospital* II (July 1953), 148–151. Cited in Haynal, 32.

11. Martindale C. Father, "Absence, Psychopathology, and Poetic Eminence," *Psychological Reports* 31, no. 8 (1972): 43–47. Cited in Haynal, 32.

12. Ibid.

13. Carpenter, *Tolkien: A Biography*, 29.

14. *The Fellowship of the Ring*, Book I, chapter 4: "A Short Cut to Mushrooms" (New York, Ballantine Books, 1955), 122, 123.

15. Carpenter, *Tolkien: A Biography*, 29.

16. Joseph Pearce, *Literary Giants, Literary Catholics* (Fort Collins, CO: Ignatius Press, 2005), 241.

17. Letter to Michael George Tolkien, January 6, 1965, in Carpenter, *The Letters of J. R. R. Tolkien*, 353, 354.

CHAPTER 2

1. Carpenter, *Tolkien: A Biography*, 33.

2. Humphrey Carpenter says that part of the reason for going to St. Philip's was that it was not as costly. However, he does not explain if the sponsor was asking Mabel to find a more economical school or if he had stopped supporting her at some point.

3. Michael White, *Tolkien: A Biography* (New York: New American Library, 2001), 25.

4. Duriez, *Tolkien and C. S. Lewis*, 7.

5. Carpenter, *Tolkien: A Biography*, 36, 37.

6. Daniel Grotta, *J. R. R. Tolkien: Architect of Middle Earth* (Philadelphia: Running Press, 1976), 26.

7. Haynal, "Childhood Lost and Recovered," 32.

8. Letter to Michael Tolkien, March 18, 1941, in Carpenter, *The Letters of J. R. R. Tolkien*, 54.

9. Donald DeMarco, *The Many Faces of Virtue* (Steubenville, OH: Emmaus Road, 2000), 217.

10. Carpenter, *Tolkien: A Biography*, 40.

11. Father Gerard Tracy, "Tolkien and the Oratory," Oratory Birmingham, accessed November 9, 2009, http://www.birmingham -oratory.org.uk/TheOratory/Tolkien/tabid/76/Default.aspx.

12. Carpenter, *Tolkien: A Biography*, 40.
13. Tracy, "Tolkien and the Oratory."
14. Carpenter, *Tolkien: A Biography*, 41.
15. White, *Tolkien: A Biography*, 37.
16. Letter to Christopher Tolkien, July 11, 1972, in Carpenter, *The Letters of J. R. R. Tolkien*, 421.
17. Ibid., 44.
18. Douglas A. Anderson, *Tales Before Tolkien: The Roots of Modern Fantasy* (New York: Del Rey, 2005), 229.
19. Letter to W. H. Auden, June 7, 1955, in Carpenter, *The Letters of J. R. R. Tolkien*, 213.
20. Helge Kåre Fauskanger, "Tolkien's Not-So-Secret Vice," Ardalambion, http://folk.uib.no/hnohf/vice.htm. Fauskanger has constructed the Ardalambion website devoted to Tolkien's many languages: https://folk.uib.no/hnohf/.
21. Carpenter, *Tolkien: A Biography*, 41.
22. Ibid.
23. John Garth, *Tolkien and the Great War: The Threshold of Middle-earth* (New York: Mariner Books, 2003), 4.
24. Ibid.
25. Ibid., 15.
26. Ibid., 16.
27. Ibid.
28. Ibid.
29. Letter to W. H. Auden, June 7, 1955, in Carpenter, *The Letters of J. R. R. Tolkien*, 213.
30. Ibid.
31. *The Return of the King*, Book VI, chapter 5, "The Steward and the King" (New York: Ballantine Books, 1955), 259.

CHAPTER 3

1. The situation is related in Carpenter, *Tolkien: A Biography*, 47. I have added some imagined conversational details.
2. Carpenter, *Tolkien: A Biography*, 49.
3. Michael D. C. Drout, *J. R. R. Tolkien Encyclopedia: Scholarship and Critical Assessment* (New York: Routledge, 2006), 244.

4. Ibid., quoting from Carpenter, *The Letters of J. R. R. Tolkien*, 43.

5. Carpenter, *Tolkien: A Biography*, 50.

6. Pearce, *Tolkien: Man and Myth*, 32.

7. Carpenter, *Tolkien: A Biography*, 52.

8. Garth, *Tolkien and the Great War*, 73. See also Drout, *J. R. R. Tolkien Encyclopedia*, 54–55.

9. Garth, *Tolkien and the Great War*, 5.

10. Drout, *J. R. R. Tolkien Encyclopedia*, 635.

11. Leslie Jones, *J. R. R. Tolkien: A Biography* (New York: Greenwood Press, 2003), 20.

12. Drout, *J. R. R. Tolkien Encyclopedia*, 635.

13. Jones, *J. R. R. Tolkien: A Biography*, 20.

14. Drout, *J. R. R. Tolkien Encyclopedia*, 135.

15. Ibid., 241.

16. Jones, *J. R. R. Tolkien: A Biography*, 20.

17. Letter to W. H. Auden, June 7, 1955, in Carpenter, *The Letters of J. R. R. Tolkien*, 214.

## Chapter 4

1. Carpenter, *Tolkien: A Biography*, 62. This event was recounted by Tolkien, though some of the details are an imaginary reconstruction.

2. Ibid.

3. Ibid. The details of this story with the company of G. B. Smith and the use of motor buses means this particular evening had to have occurred later in Tolkien's Oxford student days rather than earlier where Carpenter quotes from Tolkien's letter about the event.

4. Carpenter, *Tolkien: A Biography*, 60.

5. Jones, *J. R. R. Tolkien: A Biography*, 26.

6. Carpenter, *Tolkien: A Biography*, 60, 61.

7. Ibid., 89.

8. I originally read about the discrepancy from Clyde S. Kilby, *Tolkien and the Silmarillion* (Colorado Springs: Harold Shaw Pub., 1976), 8. However, according to one source, Kilby mistakenly attributes the quotation to a letter from Tolkien to

Vera Chapman as written in September 1973. In fact, the letter was published in the September 1973 issue of *MYTHPRINT*. The letter was not sent to Vera Chapman (the founder of the Tolkien Society, who also had a letter printed in the same issue) but to Joan O. Falconer. The letter was dated as "late 1964." A comment in a Tolkien blog provides the correct citation and a lengthier quotation used above: John D. Rateliff, "Frozen Custard, Tolkien Manuscripts, and Old Friends," *Sacnoth's Scriptorium* (blog), June 30, 2009, accessed November 16, 2009, http://sacnoths.blogspot.com/2009/06/frozen-custard-tolkien-manuscripts-and.html.

9. Carpenter, *Tolkien: A Biography*, 133.
10. Letter to Christopher Tolkien, April 18, 1944, in Carpenter, *The Letters of J. R. R. Tolkien*, 72.
11. Letter to W. H. Auden, June 7, 1955, in Carpenter, *The Letters of J. R. R. Tolkien*, 214.
12. Carpenter, *Tolkien: A Biography*, 61.
13. Ibid., 62.
14. Garth, *Tolkien and the Great War*, 16, 30.
15. Ibid., 31.
16. Carpenter, *Tolkien: A Biography*, 68, 69.
17. Ibid., 70.
18. Garth, *Tolkien and the Great War*, 30.
19. Ibid.
20. Ibid.
21. Carpenter, *Tolkien: A Biography*, 70. Readers should keep in mind that Oxford was made up of several colleges.
22. Garth, *Tolkien and the Great War*, 30.
23. Lorena Hanley Duquin, *A Century of Catholic Converts* (Huntington, IN: Our Sunday Visitor, 2003), 25.
24. Carpenter, *Tolkien: A Biography*, 73.
25. Pearce, *Tolkien: Man and Myth*, 36.
26. Ibid.
27. Ibid., 35.
28. Donald Clark Measels, *Music Ministry: A Guidebook* (Macon, GA: Smyth & Helwys Publishing, 2003), 43.

29. Carpenter, *Tolkien: A Biography*, 74.

30. Ibid., 76.

31. Jones, *J. R. R. Tolkien: A Biography*, 37.

32. Ibid.

33. Carpenter, *Tolkien: A Biography*, 77.

34. Garth, *Tolkien and the Great War*, 58.

35. Ibid., 59.

36. Ibid., 65.

37. Jones, *J. R. R. Tolkien: A Biography*, 43; Carpenter, *Tolkien: A Biography*, 81.

38. Garth, *Tolkien and the Great War*, 105.

39. Ibid.

40. Ibid., 106.

41. Anderson, *Tales Before Tolkien: The Roots of Modern Fantasy*, 22.

CHAPTER 5

1. Garth, *Tolkien and the Great War*, 44. Leslie Jones cites Modris Eksteins, *Rites of Spring: The Great War and the Birth of the Modern Age* (New York: Mariner Books, 2000), 100.

2. Garth, *Tolkien and The Great War*, 42.

3. Ibid.

4. Ibid., 137.

5. Ibid.

6. Ibid., 44.

7. Carpenter, *The Letters of J. R. R. Tolkien*, 8.

8. Ibid.

9. Drout, ed., *J. R. R. Tolkien Encyclopedia*, 713.

10. Carpenter, *Tolkien: A Biography*, 86.

11. Garth, *Tolkien and the Great War*, 134.

12. Jones, *J. R. R. Tolkien: A Biography*, 45.

13. Quoted in Garth, *Tolkien and the Great War*, 138.

14. Carpenter, *Tolkien: A Biography*, 85.

15. Ibid., 89.

16. Jones, *J. R. R. Tolkien: A Biography*, 46.

17. Garth, *Tolkien and the Great War*, 157.

18. Ibid.

19. Ibid.

20. *The Two Towers*, Book IV, chapter 2, "The Passage of the Marshes" (New York, Ballantine Books, 1955), 277.

21. Letter to L. W. Forster, December 31, 1960, in Carpenter, *The Letters of J. R. R. Tolkien*, 303.

22. Garth, *Tolkien and the Great War*, 185.

23. Ibid., 200.

24. Ibid. With details provided by Carpenter, *Tolkien: A Biography*, 93.

25. Carpenter, *Tolkien: A Biography*, 93.

26. Ibid., 93, 94.

27. Ibid., 92.

28. Garth, *Tolkien and the Great War*, 8.

29. Ibid., 8, 9.

30. Hans-Herman Hoppe, *Democracy: The God That Failed; The Economics and Politics of Monarchy, Democracy, and Natural Order* (New Brunswick, NJ: Transaction Press, 2001), ix.

31. Ibid.

32. Carpenter, *The Letters of J. R. R. Tolkien*, 188. This was in a draft to reply to a Roman Catholic who was asking Tolkien some questions about how he viewed his creative work in relation to his theology. He wrote a note on the draft that it was never sent because he thought it "seemed to be taking myself too importantly" (p. 196).

33. See Garth, *Tolkien and the Great War*, 76–78.

34. "On Fairy-Stories," reprinted in Christopher Tolkien, ed., *The Monsters and the Critics and Other Essays* (London: George Allen & Unwin, 1983).

35. Carpenter, *Tolkien: A Biography*, 103.

CHAPTER 6

1. Jones, *J. R. R. Tolkien: A Biography*, 49.

2. Garth, *Tolkien and the Great War*, 249.

3. Ibid.

4. Jones, *J. R. R. Tolkien: A Biography*, 55.

5. Carpenter, *Tolkien: A Biography*, 108.

6. Jones, *J. R. R. Tolkien: A Biography*, 55.

7. Carpenter, *Tolkien: A Biography*, 108.

8. Ibid.

9. Ibid., 109.

10. Jones, *J. R. R. Tolkien: A Biography*, 55.

11. I haven't found this explicitly stated, but Michael was born on a Friday, and it is established that Tolkien lived in Leeds during the week and then traveled down to visit the family on the weekend.

12. Jones, *J. R. R. Tolkien: A Biography*, 55.

13. Carpenter, *Tolkien: A Biography*, 111.

14. Ibid.

15. Carpenter, *The Letters of J. R. R. Tolkien*, 12.

16. Ibid.

17. Ibid., 13.

18. See Pieter Collier, "Songs for the Philologists," Tolkien Library, http://www.tolkienlibrary.com/reviews/songsforthephilologists.htm.

19. Drout, *J. R. R. Tolkien Encyclopedia*, 3.

20. Jones, *J. R. R. Tolkien: A Biography*, 61.

21. Carpenter, *Tolkien: A Biography*, 113–114.

22. Jones, *J. R. R. Tolkien: A Biography*, 61.

23. Carpenter, *Tolkien: A Biography*, 114.

24. White, *Tolkien: A Biography*, 108.

25. Ibid.

26. Ibid., 111.

27. David Friedman, "Private Creation and Enforcement of Law: A Historical Case," David D. Friedman's Home Page (website), accessed December 14, 2009. http://www.daviddfriedman.com/Academic/Iceland/Iceland.html. Originally published in *Journal of Legal Studies* 8, no. 2 (March 1979): 399–415, https://doi.org/10.1086/467615.

28. This and more are summarized in "The Influence of European Mythology on Tolkien's Middle Earth," ColorQ World, http://www.colorq.org/articles/article.aspx?d=lore&x=K_V_Tol.

29. White, *Tolkien: A Biography*, 127. White lists him as one of the more language-savvy professors in the group.

## Chapter 7

1. White, *Tolkien: A Biography*, 115, 116.
2. Ibid., 116.
3. Ibid., 123.
4. Jones, *J. R. R. Tolkien: A Biography*, 69.
5. *The American Heritage Dictionary of the English Language*, 4th ed. (New York: Houghton Mifflin Company, 2009).
6. Carpenter, *Tolkien: A Biography*, 143.
7. Ibid., 142.
8. His full name was repetitively Henry Victor Dyson Dyson, but he commonly went by Hugo Dyson for obvious reasons.
9. Duriez, *Tolkien and C. S. Lewis*, 54.
10. White, *Tolkien: A Biography*, 128.
11. Humphrey Carpenter, *The Inklings: C. S. Lewis, J. R. R. Tolkien, Charles Williams and Their Friends* (New York: Boston: Houghton Mifflin, 1977).
12. White, *Tolkien: A Biography*, 148.
13. "Roverandom" is found in *Tales from the Perilous Realm* (New York: Houghton Mifflin Harcourt, 2008).
14. J. R. R. Tolkien, *The Father Christmas Letters* (Boston: Houghton Mifflin, 1976), Year 1933.
15. White, *Tolkien: A Biography*, 152.
16. Jones, *J. R. R. Tolkien: A Biography*, 91.
17. Christopher Tolkien, ed., *The Monsters and the Critics and Other Essays* (London: George Allen & Unwin, 1983).
18. White, *Tolkien: A Biography*, 154.
19. Ibid.

## Chapter 8

1. Letter to Dora Marshall, in Carpenter, *The Letters of J. R. R. Tolkien*, 209.
2. Ibid.
3. Carpenter, *The Letters of J. R. R. Tolkien*, 27.
4. Ibid., 29.
5. Ibid., 34.
6. Ibid., 38.

7. Ibid., 40.

8. Ibid., 41.

9. Carpenter, *Tolkien: A Biography*, 192.

10. Carpenter, *The Letters of J. R. R. Tolkien*, 41.

11. Carpenter, *Tolkien: A Biography*, 192.

12. Carpenter, *The Letters of J. R. R. Tolkien*, 70.

13. Jones, *J. R. R. Tolkien: A Biography*, 97.

14. White, *Tolkien: A Biography*, 142.

15. Carpenter, *The Letters of J. R. R. Tolkien*, 115.

16. Carpenter, *Tolkien: A Biography*, 208.

## CHAPTER 9

1. Carpenter, *Tolkien: A Biography*, 218.

2. White, *Tolkien: A Biography*, 217.

3. Carpenter, *Tolkien: A Biography*, 227.

4. J.R.R. Tolkien Collection, Marquette University, Department of Special Collections and University Archives, https://www.marquette.edu/library/archives/tolkien.php.

5. Ibid.

6. Carpenter, *Tolkien: A Biography*, 238, 239.

7. Carpenter, *The Letters of J. R. R. Tolkien*, 341.

8. Carpenter, *Tolkien: A Biography*, 232.

9. Ibid., 233.

10. Kilby, *Tolkien and the Silmarillion*, 22.

11. Carpenter, *The Letters of J. R. R. Tolkien*, 341.

12. Kilby, *Tolkien and the Silmarillion*, 19.

13. Carpenter, *Tolkien: A Biography*, 253.

## CHAPTER 10

1. On May 19, 2010, fantasy author John Flanagan spoke at the St. Louis County Library. Besides discussing influences on his writing, Flanagan said that he occasionally meets with a group of fantasy authors in Sydney, Australia, who call themselves "the Drinklings."

2. See the interview in *El País* magazine: Juan Cruz, "Ser invisible . . . eso sería lo más," February 7, 2008, http://www

.elpais.com/articulo/cultura/Ser/invisible/seria/elpepicul
/20080208elpepicul_1/Tes. Thanks to the *Hog's Head* blog for a
translation: Travis Prinzi, "Rowling Invokes Tolkien, Talks
Literature and Politics," February 13, 2008, accessed November
18, 2010, http://thehogshead.org/rowling-invokes-tolkien-talks
-literature-and-politics-609/ (site discontinued). See also Dave
Kopel, "Deconstructing Rowling," *National Review*, June 20,
2003, http://www.nationalreview.com/articles/207279
/deconstructing-rowling/dave-kopel.

3. Gary Gygax interview with the Tolkien fan site TheOneRing.net,
May 30, 2000, http://archives.theonering.net/features/interviews
/gary_gygax.html.

4. Terry Brooks interview with TheOneRing.net, May 22, 2000,
http://archives.theonering.net/features/interviews/terry_brooks
.html.

5. Gygax interview, TheOneRing.net.

6. Waterstone's list of the top 100 books of the twentieth century
can be found on several places on the Internet, including at
"Waterstone's Books of the Century," Greatest Books (website),
https://thegreatestbooks.org/lists/180.

7. White, *Tolkien: A Biography*, 235.

8. Craig Levy, "Every Record *Lord of the Rings* Broke (& Which
Ones the Movies Still Hold)," Screen Rant, March 6, 2020,
https://screenrant.com/lord-rings-movies-records-box-office
-awards/.

9. Carpenter, *The Letters of J. R. R. Tolkien*, 63.

10. Ibid.

11. Ibid.

12. Ibid.

13. James Bryce, *Studies in History and Jurisprudence* (New York:
Oxford University Press, 1901), 1:263, https://oll-resources.s3.us
-east-2.amazonaws.com/oll3/store/titles/2003/Bryce_1370.01
_Bk.pdf.

14. *The Fellowship of the Ring*, Book II, chapter 7, "The Mirror of
Galadriel," 432.

15. Ibid.

16. Carpenter, *The Letters of J. R. R. Tolkien*, 344.

17. Shippey, *J. R. R. Tolkien: Author of the Century*, vii.
18. Ibid., 224; Rowling is only mentioned once according to the index. He speaks of her "unexpected success" and attributes it in part to the cultural appeal of British school stories. But the book doesn't seem to show an awareness of how big her sales would be.
19. Pictures of the gravestone and grave site can be found at the Wikimedia Commons, http://commons.wikimedia.org/wiki/John_Ronald_Reuel_Tolkien.
20. Letter to Christopher Tolkien, July 11, 1972, in Carpenter, *The Letters of J. R. R. Tolkien*, 463.

# APPENDIX:
# BIBLIOGRAPHICAL NOTE

Many of my sources are in the endnotes, but I wanted to single out five books that I think are especially important, helpful, and enjoyable.

Leslie Ellen Jones, *J. R. R. Tolkien: A Biography* (Westport, CT: Greenwood Press, 2003).

For anyone wanting to begin learning about Tolkien's life and literature and influence, this is the best place to begin. While it is short, it not only includes a summary of his life and work, but also explains Tolkien's situation and environment to the reader who might not know much about the horror of World War I or the nature of academic rank in the British university system. It also includes analyses of Tolkien's major works.

Humphrey Carpenter, *J. R. R. Tolkien: A Biography* (New York: Houghton Mifflin, 1977, 2000).

Written a few years after his death by an author who personally met with Tolkien, this is the authorized biography and the starting point of all research into Tolkien's life. Carpenter knows his stuff: he is also the editor of Tolkien's letters (with

Christopher Tolkien) and wrote a book about the Inklings as well. It is an indispensable book for anyone who wants to learn what there is to know about Tolkien's life. While it is written with the approval of the Tolkien estate, it does not hesitate to analyze Tolkien's weaknesses and questionable decisions as well as his gifts and good choices.

John Garth, *Tolkien and the Great War: The Threshold of Middle-earth* (New York: Mariner Books, 2005).

This is an absolutely outstanding book and an essential one to complement Humphrey Carpenter's biography. It focuses, as the title indicates, on the role of World War I in Tolkien's development as a writer. In so doing it reveals a great deal about Tolkien's high school and college years, his close group of friends, and his personality. It may be the best book on Tolkien ever written. It is not a complete biography, but it covers an area that has received too little attention. It contains a great deal of early Tolkien material.

Humphrey Carpenter, ed., *The Letters of J. R. R. Tolkien* (New York: Mariner Books, 1981, 2000).

These letters are an excellent resource not only for the sake of biographical information but also to show Tolkien as a writer of nonfiction prose. His letters reveal him as a thinker and one who would have made a great essayist and apologist if he had been inclined in that direction. The only real complaint one can make about this collection is that it mostly centers on his later years and thus does not really give one an accurate impression about his whole life.

Michael White, *Tolkien: A Biography* (New York: New
   American Library, 2001).

The original title of this book was *Critical Lives: J. R. R.
Tolkien*, and the author does declare his intention to write a more
"critical" work that delves into aspects of Tolkien's life that are
not as positive and glowing. White, however, is obviously an
admirer of Tolkien's work, and his book is well worth reading.
Though it is secondary material, like that of Jones mentioned
above, it goes into more detail. I would not recommend this as
a first biography, but it does have value for someone who wants
to try to understand Tolkien and how he became a creator of
Middle-earth.

# ABOUT THE AUTHOR

Mark Horne was born in Melbourne, Florida, but lived in Liberia, West Africa, and Kwajalein, Marshall Islands, before graduating from high school. After graduating from Houghton College in Western, New York, in 1989, Mark worked for American Vision and Coral Ridge Ministries, and coauthored two books with George Grant. After living in Nashville, Tennessee, where he worked as a writer/editor for Legacy Communications, Mark attended Covenant Theological Seminary in St. Louis and earned his MDiv degree in 1998. Mark has pastored two congregations since his seminary graduation and serves as assistant pastor at Providence Reformed Presbyterian Church in St. Louis. Mark is a prolific writer and the author of *A Layperson's Commentary on the Gospel of Mark*. Mark and his wife, Jennifer, have four children.